MORE STAMP COUNTERFEITING

The Perfect Crime

By H.K. Petschel

HKP PUBLICATIONS
Sandpoint, Idaho

HKP Publications
70 Cedar Dr.
Sandpoint, ID 83864

Printed in the United States of America
More Stamp Counterfeiting: The Perfect Crime

ISBN 978-1-879628-46-5

Cover design, text design by Laura Wahl
Keokee Co. Publishing, Inc. (www.keokee.com)

Acknowledgements

Not uncommonly what we accomplish is built on the shoulders of others. When I decided to research stamp counterfeiting, I soon discovered that the greatest resource was the philatelic press. As there is no known database, it was here and there; in digging through the old publications, I found references to counterfeit cases that over the years had been discovered in one city or another. I also found many individuals who had published their own research. These individuals would supply me with the leads that would take me into old newspaper files, court records and the National Archives. If one digs enough, piece by piece, you can begin to reconstruct the past.

Both my research and writing would be encouraged and supported by many luminaries in the philatelic world. The American Philatelic Society was always a source of encouragement and information. If you were questioning a stamp's authenticity, Mercer Bristow was always a ready and helpful reference. If I tried to list all the individuals who, at one time or another, would respond to a request, this in itself would be extensive.

A few who supported my efforts include: John Hotchner at the top of the list for encouraging my early writing and ongoing research; David Straight, an individual whom I have never met, but whose technical research on more than one occasion helped sort out one stamp from another; and Wayne Youngblood, who frequently asked, "Have you seen this stamp yet?" The list goes on and on. To all of you, all I can say is *thank you.*

Seek 'Stamp Faking' Team

Brothers Are Accused

New York, N. Y.—(AP)—Warrants were issued Tuesday for the arrest of Morris (Mickey Mouse) Barra and his brother Joseph as kingpins in a nation-wide counterfeit stamp ring.

Roy M. Cohn, assistant United States attorney, said the Barra brothers were close associates of Michael Maione, already under indictment by a federal grand jury on counterfeiting charges. He described Maione as the broker who handled distribution of phony stamps at a commission of 25c for each sheet of 100.

Cohn said Maione's arrest Aug. 2 threw the ring into such a panic that it dumped more than 8.000.000 stamps with a face value of nearly $250,000 in Bronx vacant lots.

Secret service agents, it was disclosed, were conducting a nation-wide search for the Barras.

Morris, 42, lived until recently with his wife and two children in the Bronx. He last was reported to be operating a bar in a hotel at Miami Beach, Fla. Joseph, 41, also lived recently in the Bronx.

CONTENTS

Preface

In "Stamp Counterfeiting: The Evolution of an Unrecognized Crime," I started to tell a story. It was the tale of how this criminal activity began in 1894 and evolved from being a small mom and pop crime to the full-blown operation of what we call organized crime. In this book my desire is to pick up where I left off – to tell what happened from 1940 to the present.

Counterfeiting has been with us since the dawn of time. If an item has value, it stands to reason that somewhere someone will decide to duplicate it. This could be anything – a token, a coin, a dollar bill. Whatever your target might be, it is the idea that is the same. It might even be your common, ordinary postage stamp.

As common as the crime of counterfeiting has been historically, one would think our library shelves would be filled with stories that related these misadventures. Surprisingly this has not been the case. On occasion you may read about some art forgery and, of course, currency, but who would bother to copy a stamp? Possibly they might target an item of great rarity, but a common ordinary stamp – never. That is where you are wrong. What you are forgetting is that nobody looks at a stamp. It is an item you use once and throw away. Also if your target is government revenue, you are not just printing one stamp. You are printing millions.

What I am going to present is a series of stories – true crime stores. It will tell you who did it, how they did it, and, finally, how and if they got caught. These are stamp stories, but I hope they will be of interest to more than just the stamp collector. I may not go into great detail on stamp production, but of interest for the collector, I will also relay how to tell the good stamp from the bad. What I hope to do is highlight how the revenue of the U.S. Postal Service has increasingly been under attack, and these attacks have not been insignificant. On an annual basis, they have cost the government not just millions but hundreds of millions of dollars. This activity may not be why the U.S. Postal Service has gone broke, but it surely has not helped.

The title is appropriate. Stamp counterfeiting has been the perfect crime, and individuals have made millions of dollars doing it.

If that is not significant enough, what do you do when you are under attack from another nation state? My hope is to encourage public awareness so maybe this problem can be addressed. As long as there is money to be made, it is unlikely this activity will be stopped, but just maybe with awareness we can make this crime a little more difficult to commit.

It would also help if the postal establishment would have an attitude adjustment. The loss of postal revenue to criminal activity should really not be looked upon as a revenue shrinkage problem. Do we look on the counterfeiting of our currency as a shrinkage problem? If United States postage is also to be defined as an obligation of the government, how can the loss of revenue to counterfeiting activity be called shrinkage?

1

The Quiet Before The Storm

In fits and starts postal counterfeiting cases appeared to come and go. There will be years when in the public record you find no activity. Then, all at once, usually in some insignificant news report, it will pop up again. It has been my suspicion that in those apparent periods of inactivity the counterfeiters did not go away. There simply were cases that had not been discovered. After all, who looks at your common, everyday postage stamp? The general public surely does not, and unfortunately the same must be said for the authorities. Historically, the people responsible for protecting the revenue of the U.S. Postal Service, the postal inspectors, did not go out of their way to look for counterfeiting. Generally, they waited for either citizens or some informant to knock on their door. Or better yet, maybe the Secret Service would just handle whatever was going on.

The people who frequently do look at stamps, and more importantly can tell one from another, are the collectors. An impression I have is that in 1949, it was once again a member of the stamp fraternity who came to the defense of the government. A story told by Herman Herst, the renowned philatelic author, was that a noted New York stamp dealer/collector had been approached by an individual offering to sell him a substantial quantity of stamps at a large discount. When he was given a sample for inspection he soon concluded that these items were not discounted postage; they were counterfeits. Being a good citizen, he immediately ran to the authorities. The memory of World War II was still fresh in his mind and he considered it to be his patriotic duty to report this crime was occurring. The stamp in question was the then current 3-cent Jefferson.[1]

The stamp dealer reported his concerns to the New York office of the Secret Service. When his story was evaluated the agents soon concluded it had merit. At the time what was most likely not

---

1 As we go along, I may offer tongue in cheek some rules to live by for the wannabe counterfeiter. This is a good object lesson. Unless you know the guy you are dealing with is a crook, it probably is not a good idea to sell counterfeits to your friendly local stamp dealer. Yes, there are charlatans, but dealers, by and large, are good citizens. Time and again this has been tried and promptly reported to the authorities.

recognized was that this tip would provide the agents with the key to an investigation that had been stymieing the New York agents for some time. Before the case was concluded, it would involve not only postage stamps, but also organized crime, and a major counterfeit currency case they had been chasing. Not limited to New York, the activities of this gang would have tentacles that spread over a large part of the country. If Herst's tale was correct, it was the stamps that must be credited with breaking the currency case wide open.

True to their name, the Secret Service had let little be known about the investigation. The public record gives the impression that up to this point their agents had been having limited success. They had identified and put under surveillance a number of low-level passers, but they were still trying to get the goods on who the major players were. This was not for lack of trying, and the pressure was on. Agents had been turning up bogus bills all over the East Coast. Still, the government had developed information that the currency they were chasing in the East originated in Chicago. This had to be considered a significant investigation. In the last year alone, over $1 million worth of bogus bills (identified to this source in Chicago) had turned up.

It is my belief that the break for the government occurred in New York when this stamp dealer/collector walked into the local Secret Service office. He told them the story of how he had been approached by an individual who offered him a large quantity of 3-cent presidential (Jefferson) Scott No. 807 stamps at a 50 percent discount from their face value. Just from the sales price, our stamp dealer probably knew he had to be dealing with either stolen or counterfeit stamps.[22] With no idea what they had stumbled into, the agents decided this was a good lead that needed to be followed up. It was what the Secret Service suggested next that put this good citizen on edge. They wanted him to go back to the seller and make a purchase with marked money.

Needless to say, this good citizen was less than enthusiastic about what the agents were proposing. Suddenly, when he realized they wanted him to make a deal with folks he suspected were dangerous

2 Legitimate discounted postage will commonly sell for about 90 to 95 percent of face value. Stolen stamps from, say, a burglary generally will sell for about 50 to 75 percent off. If you are paying less than 50 percent, you are probably buying counterfeit stamps. That is how it normally works in the world of counterfeits. Another angle will be presented in the last chapter.

criminals, he tried every way possible to excuse himself from the government's plan. It is one thing to volunteer information. It is another to put yourself in the line of fire. It was only much later, after the agents appealed to his patriotism, that he would relent. The agents swore to him that at every step, they would be right behind him, and he would be protected.

The stamp dealer's reluctance was very understandable. Agents, not private citizens, after all, are trained to do this type of thing. One can only imagine the nerves, sweating palms and beating heart that he must have felt when he finally walked up the stairs and knocked on the seller's door. Even veteran agents have a feeling of trepidation every time they work in an undercover capacity. One normally does not picture the image of a stamp dealer as an action figure or super hero.

For all the fear and trepidation, the deal did go down without a hitch. It probably helped that the men he was dealing with appeared to be both knowledgeable about stamps and friendly. Why wouldn't they be? After all, this was not some big drug buy they were negotiating. Nor were they dealing with some known criminal lowlife. To their mind, this buyer was just an average citizen who was open to a little larceny. Without incident, the stamps and money changed hands. Then, as soon as he exited the building, the stamp dealer was scooped up by the waiting Secret Service agents. They rapidly debriefed the buyer, verified the stamps were counterfeit and then broke into the building to arrest the occupants.

It was at this point the case took an unexpected turn. Herman Herst's reporting ended at this point, and the arrest and search that occurred on the night of August 1 was not reported in the press. What would appear in the August 3, 1949, New York Times were the results of another search and arrest. No mention was made of postal inspectors, and there was little comment on counterfeit stamps. This should be expected when the Secret Service is involved in a case. To them, counterfeit money is sexy, and stamps are not.

The assistant U.S. Attorney picked to prosecute this case would make sure it received press coverage. He was an up-and-coming young attorney who would be well known to the public. His name was Roy Cohn. In the New York office, Cohn had just made the jump from being a simple clerk-typist to that of prosecuting attorney. Knowing a good thing when he saw it, Cohn would use this and other counterfeit cases as his ticket to national prominence.

Cohn soon established a track record of spoon-feeding sensational stories to friendly reporters. In this case the newspaper's headline fed by Cohn read: "Ex-Convict Seized as Distributor of $250,000 in Bogus Cash in East." A born master of press manipulation, Cohn instinctively knew how to capture the public's attention. The story he spun was that the man arrested was a dapper ex-convict he identified as Michael Maione. It was Cohn's claim that Maione was responsible for the East Coast's distribution of counterfeit currency then flooding the country that originated in Chicago. The bills in question were the bogus "B" and "G" series seeing heavy circulation on the East Coast.

It was Cohn's request to the court that in the pending grand jury's action, Maione be held on a bond of $50,000. When the papers described this arch criminal's appearance, it would match the criminal stereotyping appearing in the tabloids of the day. When he appeared before the magistrate, Maione was dapperly attired in a well-fitting brown gabardine suit, offset with brown and white sport shoes. With counterfeit stamps well down on the priority list of the Secret Service, Maione was charged with the possession and sale of counterfeit money, and no mention was made of counterfeit stamps.

As Cohn would later be quoted in the press, "The arrest of Maione, who was seized at 11:30 as he slept in his home at 2123 Williams Bridge Road, the Bronx, was a crushing blow to counterfeiting activities throughout the nation." Then finally, as almost an afterthought, he mentioned, "Maione has also taken a leading role in the revival of the old racket of counterfeiting three-cent postage stamps." Cohn let slip that the phony stamps had appeared in New York in April. For at least five months these items may have been available for use in the mail.

According to Cohn, Maione had been under surveillance by the Secret Service for nearly a year. Yet agents had been frustrated in their attempts to build a case against him. His business was carefully conducted. It was stated that during the day Maione would meet his customers in a Bronx candy store. If business was to be conducted, it appeared these meetings would usually be after midnight and would take place in one of the neighborhood restaurants. If money were to actually change hands, this would occur either in subway stations or a parked vehicle. They believed Maione supplied counterfeit money to his distributors on a commission basis with Maione collecting anywhere from $5 to $15 for $100 in bogus bills. When questioned by agents John W. Kett and Carmine J. Motto, Maione would list his profession as a distributor of jukeboxes.

Maione was not an individual unknown to law enforcement. Police booking records would show that since 1929 this individual had been convicted of burglary, assault, robbery, as well as for policy and alcohol tax violations. He could be considered not only a career criminal, but also as a poster child for what would eventually be identified as a street-level soldier in organized crime. The job of every foot soldier in the "mob" was to make money for the bosses.

When I first encountered this story, one thing that added spice and immediately got my attention was the very name Maione. I have no idea if there was any family relationship, but the name Maione was well known in the circles of organized crime. Harry "Happy" Maione was a charter member of "Murder, Inc." Being a killer for hire, Harry is credited with the murder of at least a dozen individuals, and this number is generally considered to be a low estimate. In 1942, he would die in the Sing Sing electric chair.

As stated previously, even though it was the counterfeit stamps that broke the Secret Service investigation open, initially the stamp aspect of the case would only receive minimal coverage at best. It was a reporter's questions that pinned Cohn down and pulled more details out of him. Forced to respond, he stated that those items had only recently been on the market and were only a new development. It is my suspicion that when the Secret Service raided the building looking for stamps, they had no idea it would lead to the currency they had chased for a year. One of the men arrested must have identified Maione as being the source of the stamps they were selling.

Any thoughts that the Treasury Department, Mr. Cohn, or even the postal authorities might have had about downplaying the counterfeit stamp aspect to this case was immediately destroyed by an event on the ground. On August 6, a group of boys playing near the Bronx River made a discovery. They came across six large bundles, each wrapped in heavy brown kraft paper and tightly secured with a heavy cord. When opened, these bundles were found to contain 2 million counterfeit Jefferson stamps. The printing format was 100 stamps per page. If the bundles were stacked together, they would make a pile that would have been about a yard and a half high.

The very next day not far from the first discovery, in another vacant lot, another collection of bundles was discovered. In this second cache of parcels there were at least 5 million more stamps. This time they were in seven large burlap sacks. In each bag there were two large bundles wrapped exactly like those found the day before. One significant point that was noted with both discoveries: The abandoned stamp sheets had not yet been perforated. The obvious conclusion the authorities drew was that someone in the gang was panicking, and evidence was being dumped before the authorities moved in. Asked to describe the quality of the stamps being found, the postal authorities acknowledged that it would be hard to tell a bad stamp from the good.

On August 7, Cohn again met with reporters, and made the announcement that the investigation was officially spreading to other parts of the country. Again, the conclusion the government presented was that the counterfeit stamps may have originated in New York, but the bad currency was coming from Chicago. Trying to concentrate on the currency, Cohn tried to downplay Maione's involvement with the stamps. When pressed, he acknowledged the discarded stamps found by the river were exactly the same as the ones previously identified in this case.

The media again took notice on August 9, when what was described as a 52-year-old grandmother was taken into custody. Again, Cohn did not hesitate to give access to the press. He accused the woman now in custody of being the contact person between Maione's currency gang and underworld elements in Connecticut. When this woman made her own statement, she of course denied being involved in any criminal activity. Cohn responded that the government had established that this person was responsible for setting up a meeting between criminals from New York City and a person whom Cohn would identify as being Connecticut's public enemy No. 1. Purportedly, the purpose of this little get-together in Connecticut was to negotiate the sale and delivery of counterfeits to be distributed

Obviously Cohn had done this for show more than anything else, and it was a common tactic he would fall back on in the future. Questioned about this, he would justify his actions by saying he knew an offer had been made to Maresca to be the "chairman," to direct the distribution of stamps in the Northeast. Cohn may have known this had occurred, but it was something he would never be able to prove. This line of investigation went no further.

Not noted for half measures, the Secret Service kept digging to run down any loose ends. A question that still needed to be addressed was who made the stamps. Following the bread crumbs, on September 22, an announcement was made that three individuals had been identified as responsible for the production of 12 million counterfeit stamps. Philip Schwartz, 31, and Nicholas Fransca, 45, were immediately taken into custody. Both of these men were identified as respected family men who up to this point had no prior criminal records. They had operated a company, the Manhattan Photolith Plates, Inc., located at 19 Warren St. Amusingly enough, it was noted that this business address was just a few steps from 90 Church Street, the headquarters of the New York Secret Service.

The third suspect was identified as Saul Schackman, 35, who operated a printing shop at 120 Monticello St., in Jersey City. Schwartz and Fransca brought him the plate work and Schackman did the printing. When his business was visited by the Secret Service, they would seize a large printing press, the plates used to print the stamps, and at least half a ton of gummed paper. It was estimated that the unused paper the agents found could have produced an additional 4 million stamps. The breaks that reportedly led to those arrests may have originated with Schackman himself. It was reported that just 10 days previously he had been picked up by the FBI for his involvement with a stolen car gang. It was just the day after his release on that charge that the Secret Service moved in. Think this was a coincidence? I don't think so.

Cohn told the reporters these men had been under surveillance for a number of weeks. The two agents Cohn credited with masterminding this investigation were John W. Kett and Carmine J. Motto. He stated they had been chasing down the bogus currency for over a year. [3] Those agents had to be credited with putting all the pieces together, not only in the currency case but now in the counterfeit stamps case as well. What would never be mentioned was that it was the offer made to sell stamps to the New York stamp dealer that provided the key used to unlock their currency case.

When the New York Times finally did comment on the original stamp purchase, they wrote that the first inroad the agents had was the undercover purchase of 1,000 sheets of stamps made by an agent from a distributor. Most likely this was the purchase made by our stamp dealer/collector, which in turn led to the arrest of Michael Maione. If the stamp dealer/collector saw this account, most likely he was surprised to learn he had been promoted to the status of agent.

By September 24, the Secret Service cleared up any questions that remained on the perforation of the stamps. They charged Peter and Angelina Buscemi with negotiating the purchase of a modern perforating machine used in this crime. Originally the suspects had been using an old single line perforator that was found to be inadequate for the job that had to be accomplished. This old machine simply could not put out the volume of perforated stamp sheets that was necessary. When the stamp perforation was finished, the bogus stamps were picked up by the Barra brothers who in turn made the delivery to Maione.

By October 1, 1949, a new set of indictments came down, this time charging 18 individuals. Within five months all of these prosecutions would be completed. Well, this was with the exception of one suspect who was still in the wind. When the arrests began, this individual had fled to Mexico after dyeing his hair and growing a mustache; he would spend the next year working on a fishing boat. After a year went by, he must have concluded that things had cooled down enough for his return. When his plane landed in New York, the FBI was waiting. Meanwhile, in court, the designated ringleader, Michael Maione, had been sentenced to three years. Many of the other defendants received suspended or very minor sentences. Joseph Barra received the stiffest sentence – five years.

3 This is an advantage that federal agents have over local law enforcement. You can work your case for as long as it takes. In just about every metro police department at any given moment you have about 30 cases piled up on your desk. You either clear a case fast or close it. That is why there are so many cold case files.

In one of the final press reports wrapping up the details, an interesting comment was found. The source for this was Assistant U.S. Attorney John C. Hilly. He again identified the source of the currency as Chicago. Then he went on to say that Maione's organization had flooded the East with $1 million worth of $10 and $20 bills. What was significant was the next part. He commented that in the last year this same Chicago press that printed the currency had also put out $500,000 worth of counterfeit stamps. Was this a mistake or the identification of another stamp case that the public knew nothing about? For all those members of the stamp collecting fraternity who over the years have argued that nobody would counterfeit a simple postage stamp to defraud the government, they should think again. One thing is known. There is no public record that the Chicago press that reportedly was producing both currency and now stamps has ever been identified.

As stated before, if one simply followed the news coverage, it would seem as though the postal inspectors had little or no involvement in this investigation. In the reports I found, never once are they mentioned or given any credit. Then, one day while poking around files in the Inspection Service Washington Crime Laboratory, I found a collection of the Jefferson stamps, both counterfeit and genuine. This material had possibly been prepared as a court exhibit. Along with the stamps was a case summary from which the following excerpt is taken:

Huge counterfeit stamp ring smashed

> Excellent work on the part of Secret Service agents and Post Office Inspectors L. J. Bader and R. H. Kemper ably assisted by New York City Police has resulted in the smashing of the most extensive ring of stamp counterfeiters in the history of the Postal Service. The breakup of the ring was most opportune, coming just at the time when the counterfeiters were preparing to flood the country with bogus 3-cent stamps.
>
> The scheme was planned by two brothers, Morris (Mickey Mouse) Barra and Joseph Barra, for whom arrest warrants have been issued, and who have long prison records. It had originally been decided to dispose of the stamps in European and Asiatic countries but this plan was discarded and plans were made for the distribution of the stamps by one Mike

> Maione who, it is believed, directed the operations of a gang which is responsible for passing about $1,000,000 a year in fake $10 and $20 bills on the East Coast. However, less than a week after Maione's arrest on August 2, 5,000,000 stamps were abandoned by the gang in vacant lots in the Bronx. Altogether a total of 10,000,000 stamps were printed and efforts are being made to locate the missing stamps.

That last statement was significant. It would seem that maybe 5 million stamps were unaccounted for. Thinking of this, I can only remember the thousands of Jefferson stamps I destroyed as a kid because they were duplicates in stamp mixtures.

Description of 3-cent Jefferson
Scott No. 807

This stamp was a photographic reproduction and most likely printed from lithographic plates. The stamps were printed in sheets of

100 stamps each with no marginal markings. There are no plate block numbers on the individual sheets. The top and bottom margins are wider than the side margins. To the casual observer, this stamp would pass as genuine with no suspicion. It was said that to an experienced stamp collector, the counterfeit nature of these items would be apparent. The stamps of the presidential issue of 1938 of which this counterfeit is a copy were perforated 11 inches by 10.5 inches. The perforation on the counterfeits seized by the government is 12. Originally the perforations on the counterfeit were ragged and not cleanly done because they had been run off on inferior equipment. A second perforator was obtained, the technical details of which are not known. Imperforated examples of this counterfeit exist because large quantities of these items were dumped before the government's agents moved in. It is also believed a large number of the imperforated sheets simply never made it into the government's seizure inventory. That the counterfeit Jefferson stamps would pass undetected through the mail was aptly demonstrated by Assistant U.S. Attorney Cohn. He used a number of these items on his personal correspondence.[4]

The Person I Suspect Made the Undercover Buy And Wrapping Things Up

The private citizen who came forward to alert the Secret Service about the existence of the counterfeit stamps, and who subsequently was used by them to break the case open, has never been publicly identified. In the official reports and general press coverage, both the Secret Service and the postal inspectors referred to the purchase being made by an "agent." It is my personal suspicion that the person whose identity was being protected was in fact George B. Sloane. I have no factual basis for this but have simply noted that Sloane appeared to have an inside track when it came to information on this and many other counterfeiting cases. The person who related the story of the stamp buy was Herman Herst, a close associate and friend of George Sloane's.

After the purchase was made and the raid went down, Sloane, or whoever, turned the stamps over to the Secret Service. Innocently,

4 "Citizen Cohn," Nicholas Van Hoffman, Doubleday, p77

he then asked the agents if he could keep one of the sheets as a memento of his adventure. He was disappointed when the agents declined his request. Later that night, when he was back in his house, he remembered during the negotiations he had been given a block of stamps to keep as a souvenir. Without thought he had slipped those stamps into his pocket. Upon reflection he decided he would not mention his discovery to the Secret Service.

Over the years, a number of these items have made their way into the philatelic marketplace. I have a photograph of a mailing piece in a private collection postmarked Grand Central Station in 1949. Also noted was a fully gummed imperforate block of 16 stamps offered in the McBride stamp auction of May 1992. This block of stamps sold for $260. In January of 1961, Herman Herst Jr. related how he had seen even more copies of the 3-cent Jefferson. A prominent New York collector had shown him a complete sheet he had obtained. This last item was accompanied with a letter from Postmaster General James A. Farley presenting the sheet to the collector with an explanation on their origin.[5]

Some parting thoughts are in order on Prosecutor Roy Cohn. He was a man of great drive and ability. This was aptly demonstrated by his jump from clerk-typist to Assistant U.S. Attorney. In his time in the spotlight of national events, his legacy would be as a poster boy for those who wished to cast aspersions on the legal profession. As a prosecutor he not only courted the media, he excelled at manipulating the media. When he realized that Secret Service cases were professionally investigated, time and again he would use their counterfeiting cases as stepping-stones to bigger and better things.

While in the U.S. Attorney's office he developed the bad reputation of not prosecuting cases but rather milking them for headlines. Once the press release was made, many a case would die on the vine and go no further. Through his interviews and press releases he did achieve the notoriety he desired. When he left the U.S. Attorney's office, he would go down to both fame and later infamy as the lead attorney on the Committee for Un-American Activities. His eventual disbarment was simply a part of the downward spiral that

5 In today's world one might consider something like this official corruption. Where Farley was concerned, this was simply business as usual. His history as Postmaster General is replete with stamp adventures of questionable legality.

eventually consumed him.

An example of how Cohn manipulated the press and used publicity to his own ends can be demonstrated in how he handled one organized crime investigation. In this case it was not counterfeit stamps that reportedly drew the attention of the government. This case involved actual legitimate postage stamps used in a fraud. In the New York Times the headline appeared: "U.S. to investigate affairs of Adonis."

In the tabloids, Joseph "Joe Adonis" Doto had been identified as both a wealthy gambler and as a recognized criminal figure on the streets of New York. Though Adonis had started life as a penniless street urchin, through his criminal activities he had moved up the food chain in the world of organized crime. Now he was one of the wealthiest men in the United States. He sat on "The Commission" with Lucky Luciano and was directly responsible for directing the activities of Albert Anastasia and his Murder, Inc., crew. If someone needed to be killed, it was Adonis who gave the word.

Even from his position of wealth and prominence, it was well known that Adonis continued to dabble in "ordinary" criminal activity. Some individuals are simply criminals at heart. He first came to the attention of Roy Cohn when Adonis' brother-in-law would be implicated in the counterfeiting of $400,000 in traveler's checks, described later in this chapter.[6] This case went away when the government's two primary witnesses suddenly disappeared.

Cohn would haul Adonis before a federal grand jury not for any connection with that crime but rather for his suspected involvement with the stamp fraud activity of Harold Ambrose. That individual was a special assistant to the Postmaster General. When Adonis appeared before the grand jury to testify, he refused to answer any questions. Ambrose would not be so lucky. He would be charged with accepting money from investors as part of a scheme he had dreamed up that involved commemorative stamps. Reportedly he had made the representation to various investors that he could manipulate the supply of given commemorative stamps, and he would thus be able to inflate their value as an investment. Adonis professed that his only involvement in what had gone down was as a victim. His story was that he innocently invested $125,000 with Ambrose, and for his

6 In printer's waste while investigating the Jefferson stamp, Agent Motto found evidence of traveler's checks. Could these have been the same ones?

efforts he had only received back $20,000.

Ambrose would plead guilty to one count out of a 22-count indictment, and he would be sentenced to serve from two to seven years. He was released from federal custody in February 1951, after serving just the minimum sentence. It is not really known what Adonis' degree of involvement actually was. If he truly were the real mastermind behind this scheme, Adonis surely would not say so. Ambrose was bright enough not to say anything either. Then again, maybe Joe was simply an innocent stamp investor, and I have a bridge I would like to sell you. That organized crime would get involved in a scheme that related to the Post Office should not come as a surprise to anyone either. As a criminal organization they have long looked upon the Post Office and the revenue it generated as a piggy bank. Why would you think they would look upon stamps that had collector interest as being any different?

Then There Is Another Version of the 3-Cent Jefferson Story

With any criminal case, information the public can glean from news reports is frequently only a part of the story. If you happen to be a cop, you might get the full story late at night on some stakeout or when you are unwinding in some after-hours cop bar. That is when one frequently hears what really went down in a particular case.

A good example of how different versions of the same story can exist was amply demonstrated with this 3-cent Jefferson case. I did not have the benefit of sharing some boring, late-night surveillance or, better yet, some smoky bar with Agent Motto, but there was an unexpected development. After Motto retired from a distinguished career in the Secret Service, he took up writing. His first book, "Undercover" is a textbook on how to conduct clandestine investigations. In his second book, "In Crime's Way," he offered a montage of some of the investigations he had been involved in over the years. One of the stories he touches on was the 3-cent Jefferson. A problem this presents is that in this published rendition he gives a very different presentation of events than what was found in the newspapers. Frequently I asked myself if this was the same story I had pieced together from news clippings.

In Motto's book I did find the answer to one question that had bothered me. From day one it had been my suspicion that this was an organized crime case, but this was a term of reference that was not recognized or commonly used at that time. Then in the book I found Motto visiting with Joseph Valachi[7] in his prison cell. Motto's motivation for his visit was to see if Joe could give him information on any of his cold counterfeit cases. For his part, all Valachi really wanted to do was gab about the old days. It turned out that the Jefferson stamp case came up in their conversation.

"Yeah, I remember. You cleaned out the neighborhood. For a while, things were getting pretty bad: No one knew who was going to be picked up next. There was even talk of getting you," Valachi said.

It was never identified who was gunning for Motto, but it is my suspicion that good candidates would be either Maione or one of the Barra brothers. Then in a chapter he titled, "Postmarked from Prison," Motto presented another version of the stamp story. According to Motto, his big break occurred one day when he was in the office just trying to catch up on case paperwork. A middle-aged woman walked in and with a little prodding told him an interesting story.

Reluctantly she told Motto her sister, whom she described as a "knockaround" woman, was hanging out with a rough crowd. Her sister had asked her if she knew anyone who would be interested in buying counterfeit stamps.[8] To demonstrate to Motto that this was for real, and not some story she was just making up, the woman then produced a 3-cent stamp. It took Motto some time to conclude that, yes, this stamp was counterfeit.

A complication that Motto introduced with his book was that he changed the names. This was not to protect the innocent but rather the guilty. His thinking was that these individuals had paid their debt to society. The problem this presented was trying to figure out who in his book matched up to who was in the press reports.

In his book, Motto would call the sister of his walk-in informant

---

7 Joseph Valachi was a low-level Mafia soldier who, to avoid the chair, would testify before the McClellen Committee, Bobby Kennedy and national TV. He would publicly blow the lid off of organized crime in the United States. Before the cameras he told how the families were organized and how one became a member of the Mafia. J. Edgar Hoover was finally forced to recognize that, yes, there was such a thing as organized crime in the United States.

8 This woman's real problem with her sister was not counterfeit stamps; she was having an affair with her husband.

"Brenda." This woman was not an individual who normally would be cooperating with authorities. Motto knew neither of these women would normally be cooperative with law enforcement, and there had to be an ulterior motive at work here. Still he had a counterfeit stamp, and this was something that needed to be followed up. He decided that he would have one sister introduce him to the other as a potential buyer. He picked the main lobby of the Post Office as the location for this get-together.

When "Brenda" showed up, she was accompanied by two hoods Motto described as looking like fugitives from a Cagney movie. They were wearing dark suits, dark shirts, white ties and had hats pulled down over their eyes. You cannot make this stuff up. The negotiations occurred, and after a lot of going back and forth, a price of $1.50 per sheet was finally agreed on.

Back at the office, when Motto ran what he was doing past his boss, the general consensus was that neither of them could imagine why anyone would have gone to the bother of duplicating a common postage stamp. Possibly with some reluctance Motto's boss authorized him to go ahead. Still, he was given firm instructions not to lose any of the government's money. With that in mind, Motto returned to the Post Office where he dragged his brother into the mix. His brother just happened to be a postal inspector, so at least in this case inter-agency cooperation existed from the beginning.

Drafted into the playacting, the role Motto's brother assumed was that of a postal clerk. The story they put forth was that these stamps could be slipped in with good postage and sold out of Post Office stamp windows. They said they might even be able to go a step further. The stamps could be used to fill overseas orders where surely they would never be discovered. Can you say that greed probably overcame common sense? With dreams of riches before her, "Brenda" agreed to sell the agents several thousand sheets of stamps. While making this agreement, she warned Motto that he better not be pulling anything funny, because there were some "big people" behind this deal. Everything had better go as planned or there would be problems, she warned.

When the stamp buy finally went down, Motto and his brother met with "Brenda" and her two shadows. After the money changed hands, Motto opened the trunk of his car supposedly to deposit the stamps. That was the signal he had set up for his watching agents to move in and make the arrests.[9] Now with 6,000 sheets of stamps in his possession and three individuals in custody, Motto knew this case was still far from over. In the negotiations, "Brenda" had informed him there could be at least 5 million more counterfeit stamps available for sale. Brought into the act, the Post Office soon verified that this was not a one-time affair. Inspectors checking incoming Christmas mail soon found some of these counterfeit stamps going through the mail.

When Motto tried to get information from the folks he had in custody, it was soon apparent that no one was in any hurry to talk, and Motto continued his investigation. One big clue you have with either currency or stamps is the paper being used by the offenders. Motto sent 10 sheets of the stamps to the director of the Gummed Paper Institute for their examination. He reasoned that if he could identify the paper being used, just maybe he could figure out who the seller was, and then with luck, the buyer. While this went on, "Brenda" sat in jail and was getting madder and madder by the day. Her two buddies had soon been bailed out, but in more than three weeks nobody came to her rescue. Finally she reached out to Motto and told him she wanted to talk.

The story "Brenda" told Motto was that she had first heard about counterfeit stamps from an old friend she identified as "Chet." He was her connection to the stamps and was looking for distributors. She had told Chet that she had another friend in Connecticut whom she believed might be interested in these stamps. They even made a trip there to meet this person (Maresca), but apparently no deal had been reached. Then in talking to Motto she dropped a bomb. She told Motto that "Chet's" nickname was "the Mouse." Motto knew who "the Mouse" was - read Maione - and that he was connected to the Mafia. "The Mouse" was already under suspicion as the primary East Coast distributor for counterfeit currency.

About the same time Motto discovered he was dealing with "the Mouse," the report from the Gummed Paper Institute arrived at his door. This report revealed not only the type of paper being used, but also the hundred or so distributors of this product in New York City.

9 I laughed when I read this. Years later I was using the same signal in my own undercover buys.

The paper was identified as "Perfection White," and the manufacturer had put a chemical marker in the mucilage that had enabled the exact press run to be identified. Provided with this list, Motto began the tedious job of visiting each and every one of these businesses. Frustrating days lay ahead until, one day, he walked into a rundown printing supply business on the lower East Side.

When he walked in the front door at "Front's Supplies," he must have thought this was going to be another dead end. His immediate impression was this was anything but a thriving business. The counter was broken, papers were scattered all over the floor, and just about everything was covered with dust and cobwebs. After banging around the office for some time, he finally found the owner dozing in a back room. Motto did not hold out a lot of hope that anything would come out of this visit, but lo and behold, the proprietor did remember selling "Perfection White" paper. Then searching through scattered papers for about half an hour the shop owner eventually found not only the invoice for the sale of 10 reams of "Perfection White," but also the bounced check that went with this sale.

The people behind this criminal enterprise, or at least those who were identified as the major distributors, may have been professional criminals, but it soon became obvious the person doing the printing was not. Motto ran a name check and determined that this person was unknown to law enforcement.[10] The agent decided that with this individual his best approach was to simply meet the guy and then see what would happen. Not sure of what to expect, he went to the address of record and introduced himself to "Manny Epstine."

Motto used a very low-key approach. He simply drove up to the print shop by himself and, after introducing himself, asked Manny if he had purchased any "Perfection White" paper. When the suspect responded no, Carmine then showed him a copy of his bounced check. Caught in a lie, if Manny had not been nervous before, at that point he must have been in almost a total panic or collapse. Settling him down, Motto suggested that this need not be the end of Manny's world. He suggested they simply go out to dinner and talk things over. In an atmosphere that was much less confrontational,

10 This part of Motto's book was directly contradicted by the news reports at the time of the arrests.

Motto explained the facts of life. If "Epstine" cooperated just maybe things could be worked out. If he did not help the agent, he would find himself in a lot of trouble. He told Manny that a lot of people had already been picked up and others were talking. If, however, he cooperated and told the agent everything he knew, this would be made known to the court, and any help he provided would go a long way toward keeping him out of jail.

Manny eventually concluded it was in his best interest to cooperate with the agent. He laid out the story of his involvement with this criminal enterprise. He may have been the printer, but it had not been his idea. For about five years Manny had owned his own print shop, and whenever he needed plate work done he had gone to "Henry and Donato's" plate-making shop in the city. Knowing Manny from their many business dealings, these men had then approached him with the idea of doing stamps. They provided the finished printing plates, and he would do the printing. Needing money, Manny agreed but told the two he could not do the perforations. He was told not to worry; they already had someone lined up who would take over that part of the job. The total press run Manny contracted to do was for 12 million 3-cent Jefferson stamps.

The next day Motto introduced Manny to Roy Cohn. A formal statement was taken and arrest warrants were issued for Manny, Henry, Donato and Artie Bosca. This last individual had picked up the printed stamps from Manny and was responsible for getting them perforated.

When Henry had been arrested at his plate-making shop, on his person was found a rental receipt for another address. Motto went to check this location out. What he found there was a small rented room, but inside was a multilith press, rags soaked in printing ink and waste printing paper. When he showed his boss those scraps of paper that had the impression of a number of colored balls, he got another surprise. His boss exclaimed, "Congratulations, you have just solved the case we had on the counterfeit American Express Traveler's checks."

According to the version of the story Motto related in his book, it was only after these arrests had been made that a group of kids found the 8 million stamps abandoned in the Bronx. Motto and his boss may have been happy with the recovery of these stamps, and the arrests made, but in this later version there were still loose ends to tie up. Finally after many visits from his family and the agent, Artie Bosca began to cooperate.

When he began to talk, he soon implicated "the Mouse" – Maione – and his two friends, the Mariano (Barra) brothers. They had been in on this from the beginning and had fronted all the money used to set up the operation. Another individual involved was Felix Abbonda, who had the nickname of "The Student."[11] Bosca had been responsible for perforating the stamps, and he told Motto how he had been using an old, foot-powered perforator, which was both slow and killing his back. After he complained, "The Student" and "the Mouse" gave him the money to get a new machine. He dumped the old one in the Long Island Sound.

When it became evident to "the Mouse" that Motto had the goods on him and that he could be looking at hard time, he told his attorney to approach the agent and see about striking a deal. You have to realize here that until long after the assassination of President Kennedy, there were not a lot of Secret Service agents to go around. Motto did not have the resources available to chase individuals who might have gone into hiding. "The Mouse" made a proposal to Motto: If the government was not too hard on both him and his friends, just give him a date and time, and he would make sure that all the defendants were in the courtroom.

Actually, the person who possibly pushed "The Mouse" into cooperation was "The Student." For years he may have been involved in criminal activity, but he was hardly what one would call a hardened or known criminal. The way Motto described things, he came from a proud Italian family, most of whose members had no idea in what waters he had been playing in.[12] Complicating things, and as an additional inducement, "The Student's" younger sister was about to be married, and if he was not in attendance questions would be asked. As part of the deal, he asked Motto if he could possibly attend the

11 I have no idea what the true identity of "The Student" was or the role he played. I wish I did and what his later path in life was. Be you Irish or Italian, if you came from "the neighborhood" in a big city, it was not uncommon to become either a cop or a criminal.

12 The vast majority of immigrants of either Italian or Sicilian extraction wanted nothing to do with crime, be it organized or otherwise. Usually, in fact, they were the first targets of those who did turn to crime.

wedding and reception. In return he agreed to fully cooperate with the agent. Motto ran those propositions by Cohn and they agreed. Why not? "The Student" went to the wedding accompanied by Agent Motto. When at midnight the party broke up, "The Student" was escorted back to his cell.

True to Maione's word, on the date of the trial, 16 defendants appeared in court and they all entered guilty pleas. Cohn followed through on his part of the deal. Motto would relate how Cohn, without notes, had expounded for over an hour and a half, presenting to the judge the detailed involvement of each defendant. In his conclusion he recommended sentencing be no more than three to five years, even for the most egregious individuals. Considering Cohn was not only someone he respected, but also a friend, Motto would continue to defend this individual through thick and thin.

It was interesting to see the differences between what the newspapers reported and how the story would be related 20 years later in Motto's book. I only wish he would have done similar writing about some of the other stamp cases he was assigned to over the years. If one accepted his later writings as gospel, this would demonstrate the danger of believing everything one reads in the papers. Then maybe it is the other way around. Commonly, we only get part of the story.

A final note should be written about Carmine's brother, Robert Motto. He was a postal inspector and later transferred from the Inspection Service to the Secret Service. While Carmine would become a driving force in the Counterfeit Division, Robert would retire as the assistant agent-in-charge of the Secret Service Chicago office.

You Should Know Your Limitations

A Little Light Comedy

The story presented here is not about some postal counterfeit designed to defraud the government, but rather the story of a philatelic counterfeit designed to separate the stamp dealer/collector from their hard-earned currency. It is a story that has always amused me and deserves at least a small mention. It also illustrates why our jails are so full; it's not because those who are chasing the criminals are so smart but because your average criminal is just so dumb. I first related this story in NetStamps in 2007.

When you are going to take on some new endeavor, it only makes sense that you should have at least some small familiarity with whatever it is you are going to do. This should be especially true when the down side for screwing up is prison time. Now, it is agreed that the vast majority of criminals are not rocket scientists, but what happened in California in 1951 sets a new low bar for levels of stupidity. Their efforts produced one of the more comic moments in the annals of stamp counterfeiting. Their downfall as criminals came about when they decided to expand their horizons and copy a rare stamp. This was a marketplace they knew absolutely nothing about.

In the world of collectibles, the value of any given item is directly proportional to its scarcity. When such an item is presented for sale, automatically it is going to be critically examined, and its provenance must be established. The knowledgeable dealer or collector is not about to buy a high-buck item on blind faith alone. If you doubt this, slap some paint on a canvas and try to sell it as a Picasso. In this case, these two idiots picked one of the rarest masterpieces in the stamp world – the upside down biplane.

When the Bureau of Engraving and Printing had run off the biplane stamp, at some point in the production an error occurred. One sheet with four panes of 100 stamps each came off the rollers with an inverted center. This error was not discovered until Col. E.H. Green purchased one of these sheets at a Washington, D.C., post office. To my limited knowledge, the other three sheets have never been found. The value of Green's discovery had steadily climbed until, in 1950, one of these stamps had a reported value at auction of $5,000. If one of those items was offered today for $5,000, it would be snapped up in an instant.

Now, before this latest brainstorm had occurred, these two young men had been churning out $1 and $20 bills in the trailer they lived in. When they saw a story in the newspaper about this stamp, they reasoned it would be a lot easier to duplicate a stamp than the currency they had been laboring over. Their next conclusion was that if one stamp could demand such a high price, just think how much money they could make if they printed a whole bunch of these items.

Setting to work, they made their printing plate and then they ran off the bogus copies. Once they had stamps in hand, with dreams of riches they set off to peddle their wares to local stamp dealers. They thought that $4,000 per stamp would be a fair price. After many fruitless attempts to sell their masterpieces, they could not understand why they had no takers. As my youngest daughter would describe their mental capacity, the wheel may be turning, but the hamster must have been dead.

Every stamp dealer they approached summarily blew them off or simply concluded these folks were idiots and not worthy of serious attention. Apparently one dealer did listen to their spiel with some amusement and then informed them that any purchase of this significance would have to be examined and authenticated before any purchase would even be considered. Another dealer did not even attempt to be so polite. He openly expressed his skepticism and then began to ask pointed questions. He quizzed them on where and how they could have possibly acquired the items they were offering for sale. It was soon obvious that these individuals were not collectors and had no knowledge of stamps. Flustered by the cross-examination, these men would actually end up buying a few stamps from the dealer before they beat a hasty retreat out the door. Now there was a salesman. The only problem for the men was when they paid for their stamp purchase, it was with one of their homemade bogus bills.

Days later the stamp dealer was notified by his bank that he had taken in a bad $20 note. Then, not surprisingly, a few days later he had a follow-up visit from one of your friendly local Secret Service agents. Thinking back, the stamp dealer remembered the two young men and the stamps they had tried to sell him. Then he remembered something else. It was the license plate number on the car the men had been driving. He had copied it down when his suspicion had been raised. You can guess what would happen next.

2

Pick Your Friends

On October 10, 1961, federal agents arrested three men in Philadelphia, Pa for attempting to sell counterfeit 4-cent Lincoln postage stamps. This was hardly an insignificant event. More than one million stamps are known to have been involved in this attempted transaction. Two of the men in custody were identified as Joseph Anthony Costello, age 28, and his uncle, Vincent Noce, age 50. Both were residents of Brooklyn, New York. A third suspect, Peter Troiano, age 22, listed his residence as Miami, Florida. J.T. O'Keefe, the United States Attorney, described the stamps the government seized as being a "near perfect reproduction" of what the government had produced.

Joseph Jordan, chief of the Secret Service in Philadelphia, issued his own press release and he described how his agents had arrested these men after they attempted to sell counterfeit stamps to his undercover agents. The men were arrested after a stamp sale to undercover agents fell through and they were attempting to enter their vehicles to drive away. Jordan added he knew that just two weeks prior there had been an attempt to sell these same counterfeit stamps in New York City for $20,000.

The Post Office management was worried that these stamps were already on the street. After the Philadelphia arrests and stamp seizure, they sent out a warning notice that described the stamps and presented side-by-side enlarged photographs of both the counterfeit and a genuine 4-cent Lincoln. This was to alert postal employees of the existence of this counterfeit and to aid them in identifying any of these bogus items that might have already gotten into the mail system.

With news of the arrests, the stamp collecting community reacted with its typical skepticism. They promptly pooh-poohed the whole enterprise. These self-appointed stamp experts noted that stamps printed from recessed engraved plates have a sharp, clear appearance. What this means is that the inked design stands out from the paper. The stamps found in Philadelphia could best be described as flat, dull, and with a darker tone than the genuine item. The finely engraved detail from intaglio printing had been lost in the copies.

With this counterfeit, it was pointed out that the most glaring mistake was that the counterfeit had been copied from a strip of 10 stamps. The printer had photographed one stamp and then duplicated the image over and over to produce a printing plate that would produce 100 stamp images. Being copied from the coil stamp, the stamp sizing was not correct. The normal coil stamp is slightly wider than, and not quite as high as a regular issue stamp that was printed in the sheet format. If one looked closely, a person who was very knowledgeable about stamps might spot this difference, but the average citizen surely would not.

In September of 1961, an investigation had begun in New York City. An FBI informant brought in the news that stamps were going to be sold on the street. Being the FBI, and never slow to steal another agency's jurisdiction, on their own, they promptly tried to set up an undercover buy. When this sting fell through, the FBI then turned their information over to the Secret Service.

Frustrated in attempts to sell this stamp package in New York, the individuals holding these items then decided they would transport them to Pittsburgh and sell them there. In Pittsburgh, the Secret Service made an attempt to buy them there, but this undercover operation fell through when the seller had to go into hiding. He had been involved in a shooting incident and was busy trying to dodge a police dragnet. Still the Secret Service did not give up. Now working with the local postal inspectors, they were able to set up another buy attempt; this time it would be in Philadelphia.[13] They scheduled a meeting with the sellers for the night of October 9, at the Benjamin Franklin Hotel. This building was conveniently located just across the street from the local Secret Service office.

The secret for any successful undercover operation is planning and preparation. What that means is that you stack the deck in your favor so you are not only successful, but more importantly, do not get your agents killed in the process. If you want to keep your informants and agents alive, you call the shots.

13 The postal inspectors historically worked very closely with the Secret Service. With Secret Service agents being few in number, the inspectors were frequently drafted to assist with protection duties. Additionally, during election years when many agents were pulled out of field offices, postal inspectors frequently picked up their forgery investigations until local Secret Service agents returned to the field. This system came to a screeching close just before I joined the field when the Chief Postal Inspector sent the Director of the Secret Service a bill for $20,000,000 to cover inspector overtime.

Long before the sellers arrived, the agents were occupying two hotel rooms on the 12th floor, one of which they had wired for sound. On the appointed day three individuals arrived in two different vehicles and checked into Room 343. One of these men (Joseph Costello) then went up to the 12th floor and from about 9 p.m. to after 3 a.m. tried to negotiate the sale of the counterfeit postage stamps. The agents were in no hurry. They were trying to get all three of these men to implicate themselves in the crime. In an attempt to move things along after hours of frustration, Costello gave the keys to the car containing the stamps to one of the undercover agents (Agent Motto) so he could check both their quality and amount. The car containing the stamps was the one that Peter Joseph Troiano had been driving.

Considering this case had originated in New York City, it was not surprising that Agent Motto would follow it down to Philadelphia. By 1961, he was one of the premier counterfeit investigators in the Secret Service. Once he verified there actually were five boxes of stamps in the truck of the car, he then drove the vehicle across the street to the local office where agents opened and confirmed the contents. It was determined that each box contained approximately 200,000 stamps. Motto then returned the vehicle to its original location, but with one change. The Secret Service blocked it in with two of their own cars. The evidence in this case was not going anywhere.

When he returned to the hotel room, Motto had to stall the sale. The agents were still trying to get all three of the individuals involved. This they never could accomplish, and eventually in frustration the sellers would give up and decide to leave. The failure to complete the sale was deliberate on the part of the government. The United States Treasury Department really does not like to part with its money. The excuse given to Costello was when the stamps had been shown to their buyer, he was not happy with either the quality of printing or the stamp perforations.

Finally on October 10 at 3:30 in the morning the three men exited the hotel. Joseph Costello and Vincent Noce went to one car and Peter Troiano went to the one containing the counterfeit stamps. It was at this point that agents moved in and arrested all the individuals. When the prisoners were searched, Costello, who had been conducting the negotiations, was found to be carrying a revolver on his belt. Then the agents found another handgun under the driver's seat of the car he was going to drive. As for Troiano, the car he was driving was not his. It belonged to Charles San Fillippo of New York City, who was a relative of Noce's.

Now, if things had followed the normal flow of events for a criminal case, the people arrested would go to court. Maybe at some point in the future a footnote might appear in some newspaper that might mention the arrest and convictions. Two of the defendants, Costello and Noce, followed the script and entered nolo pleas. Actually they had cut a deal with the government. The third defendant, Peter Troiano, suddenly discovered that he had been nominated to be the designated fall guy and his paraphrased response was: "Hey, wait a minute. I want a trial."

Looking at the newspaper coverage given to the initial arrests, and then the subsequent prosecution, one would never suspect there had been any postal inspectors involved in bringing these individuals down. Actually, the inspectors had been intimately involved, first in New York and then with the arrests that occurred in Philadelphia. When Costello was searched after his arrest, he had Inspection Service expense money in his pocket. Still, the involvement of the inspectors would be kept to a very low profile, and given no publicity.

In Washington files a TWX message was found from the Chief Postal Inspector to the Philadelphia Inspector in Charge. In no uncertain terms it advised him that the investigative jurisdiction for counterfeit stamps rested with the Secret Service.

Still, the Post Office Department would not sit completely on its hands. A warning message was sent out. The one I found was issued on November 8, 1961, and was addressed to all postmasters in New York State:

> Recently several individuals were taken into custody at Philadelphia, Pa., with approximately one million counterfeit 4-cent postage stamps in their possession.
>
> Quantities of these counterfeit stamps were also located in different sections of New York City. It is understood that large quantities of the

stamps are in circulation throughout New York State, particularly near the Canadian border. Shown below are photographs of a genuine and counterfeit 4-cent stamp.

Counterfeit

Genuine

The Counterfeit Can Be Identified Through The Following Discrepancies:

1. They have a dark, glassy finish as compared to the flat, lighter finish of the genuine stamps.

2. Just inside the left border over Lincoln's right shoulder there is a small dark spot of white and the parallel lines are indistinct whereas in genuine stamps the lines are distinct and the dark shaded area of the top of the stamp gradually fades as it proceeds downward.

3. The hair on Lincoln's head and beard is more of a dark mass rather than the distinct lines on genuine stamps.

4. The perforations on the edges of the counterfeit stamps are of a slightly smaller diameter than those of the edges of genuine stamps.

5. Lack of detail in the printed design.

6. Difference in the printing process used.

7. Absence of parallel breaker marks normally found on adhesive side of genuine stamps.

It will be appreciated if you will disseminate the information about these counterfeit 4-cent Lincoln stamps to your employees, particularly those assigned to office letter drops and carrier collections. If any mail is discovered having the counterfeit stamps attached, please contact your nearest postal inspector or this headquarters (Pennsylvania 6-7700, ext 849) for advice. The same thing should be done if any of your window clerks should be approached regarding possible purchase or redemption of these counterfeit stamps. Kindly have anyone offering such stamps for sale or redemption identify himself. Failing in this, obtain a license plate number, should an automobile be used by the individual, and furnish a full description of him.

If you have need for additional copies of this notice in order to make further judicious distribution among your employees, please request same.

J.M. Graham
Postal Inspector in Charge

When they began to look for these items in the mail, not surprisingly, they were found. A report from New York was found dated November 15, 1961. It described how the Livorness family came into possession of counterfeit stamps. In that instance, three counterfeit stamps had been identified on letters bearing their return address. When interviewed, they claimed that a small quantity had been purchased from a dispensing machine in their local drug store. When the proprietor was interviewed he said he had received the stamps from his local milkman. When this individual was interviewed, his story was that he had found a small quantity of these items while making his regular deliveries.

The next report was dated December 12 and was from Brooklyn. Five letters bearing the counterfeit stamps had been identified in the outgoing mail. The stamps were traced back through a number of hands to a custodian who worked in a New York office building. His story was that one night he found a brown paper bag that apparently had been lost or discarded. When he looked inside, he found what he estimated were about 2,000 stamps. Before the authorities could catch up with him he stated that he had either used or sold about half of these items.

An interesting report was found dated January 5, 1962. It originated from the Elmira Reformatory:

All mail received at the Elmira Reformatory is censored. Stamps are removed from the mail before being distributed to the prisoners. One of the persons responsible for this censorship work is guard Ted Wilkinson. Mr. Wilkinson is a stamp collector, and in my conversations with him I assume well versed. Apparently because of his stamp collection activities and knowledge of stamps, Mr. Wilkinson casually examines each day all stamps which are removed from the mail. It was related that several weeks ago he detected a 4-cent stamp which gave every indication of being counterfeit. Because of having been already removed from the mailing envelope, the sender or addressee responsible could not be identified in that instance. A specific watch was immediately placed on mail to determine if any further mail should be received with counterfeit stamps.

Under date of December 29th the attached mailing envelope directed to Miguel Torres, was received. It is the opinion of Mr. Wilkinson that the 4-cent stamp on the envelope is a counterfeit. Prison records indicate that Torres receives mail approximately every two weeks, and it is believed very possible the other unidentified stamp was taken from a letter being sent to him. It is the contention of Mr. Wilkinson that this believed to be counterfeit stamp is slightly smaller than a regular stamp. In my casual observance it is apparent the texture of the paper is quite different, and the imprint lines on the stamp are blurred. The mailing envelope is referred to herewith for your information and possible association with the counterfeiting activities recently uncovered at Philadelphia. Mr. Wilkinson made the request that this envelope and affixed stamp be returned to him, if possible, when no longer needed by your service.

A report submitted by Postal Inspector A.G. Davis was found that summarized his actions in Long Island:

Mr. Edward Burkart, a truck driver for Mobil Oil Company ... found the subject counterfeit stamps. He advised that he was stopped on 31st Place, Long Island, City, N.Y., just north of Borden Avenue, when he noticed the stamps laying next to a sewer. He picked them up, took them to the Long Island City Post Office, and turned them in. He was unable to furnish any other information about them.

On October 17, 1961, collector William Golub, Southview Station, found 25 counterfeit stamps, 4-cents each, next to collection boxes located at Westchester and Ward Avenues, and 167th Street and Hoe avenue, Bronx, New York.

On October 25, 1961, Mr. Harry Ruiz, a postal clerk assigned to the Church Street Station, New York, N.Y. Post Office turned in four counterfeit stamps he had found in the vicinity of a school yard located near 171st Street and Boston Road in the Bronx. Mr. Ruiz advised that there were many more stamps on the ground and that people were picking them up. The West Farms Station was advised and sent two employees to search the area; however, no stamps were found.

Further reports were received during October and November 1961 advising that odd lots of counterfeit 4-cent stamps had been found at the intersection of 167th St., and West Farms Road, Bronx and Boynton Avenue near 174th street opposite James Monroe School. Memorandums are with the file.

On November 3, 1961, three letters were observed in the mails having counterfeit stamps. It was determined that these stamps were among a number found in the general area just north of Westchester Boulevard in the Bronx. Please see report of Postal Inspector L.B. Battles dated November 15, 12961, case No. 91126-XFL.

On November 15, 1961, a TWX from Postal Inspector in Charge – Chicago, Illinois advised that two envelopes containing 100 counterfeit postage stamps each, had been received by the Star Commonwealth Home for Boys, Albion, Michigan, as donations. The envelopes containing the stamps bore the hand-printed return cards of M. Brownel and L.M. Swan. In each case the address was 161 W. 16th St. Brooklyn, N.Y. Immediate inquiry disclosed that there was no such number on W. 16th Street in Brooklyn, N.Y. Also that these persons were unknown at 161 W. 16th New York, N.Y.

The envelopes used were return envelopes sent out by the aforementioned Star Commonwealth Home for Boys. It was noted that the return card originally placed on the envelopes was covered with Christmas seals. It was determined that the name and address which had been covered was that of Philip Guarino, 1345 Elder Avenue, Bronx, New York.

On November 10, 1961 a report was received from Postal Inspector M.H. Trumbull, Omaha, Nebraska regarding the receipt at Boys Town, Nebraska of a donation of 100 counterfeit 4-cent stamps. The envelope used was a return envelope sent by Father Flanagan's Boys' Home[14] and

14 One method the Inspection Service uses to identify potential theft problems inside the Post Office is blind testing. Every inspector was expected to mail a specific number of letters containing cash to various recipients. If these items started to disappear you knew that somewhere in the system you had a theft problem. Father Flanagan was one of the blind test addresses I had used many years later.

bore the hand-printed return card of L.M. Murphy, 161 W. 16th St., New York, N.Y. However, under the Christmas seals it was determined that the printed return card, placed on the envelope by Father Flanagan's Boys' Home prior to mailing, was that of A. LaRotunda, 1345 Elder Ave., Bronx 72, New York. It was further determined that L.M. Murphy was unknown at 161 West 16th St., New York, N.Y. and both Guarino and LaRotunda received mail at the Elder Avenue address. This information, together with the envelopes, which bore counterfeit 4-cent stamps, were subsequently turned over to Agent Motto. In turn he advised that Philip Guarino acknowledged sending the three donations, not realizing the stamps were counterfeit. He explained that he had found the stamps in the street in the vicinity of his residence. Regarding the fictitious return cards, Mr. Guarino advised that his only reason for doing that was an attempt to get his name off the mailing lists.

On December 8, 1961 five letters bearing counterfeit 4-cent postage stamps were observed in the outgoing mail at G.P.O. Brooklyn, N.Y. Your attention is invited to the report of Postal Inspector R.F. Baird and S.M. Jones, dated December 12, 1961:

During the early part of December 1961 small quantities of mail bearing counterfeit 4-cent stamps were noted in the outgoing mails at Bronx Central Station, of the New York, N.Y. Post Office. Upon advice of your office it was deemed proper that no service should be given this mail and it would be returned to sender and attempts made to determine the source of supply. A form letter was drafted and approved made by your office for use in the return of this mail. However, when this idea was presented to Mr. A. E. Whitaker, Chief, U.S. Secret Service, New York, N.Y. he advised that rather than send the counterfeit stamps back to the sender, the mail should be delivered and the counterfeit stamps retained as contraband. Agent Motto was contacted and arrangements were made to accompany him to the Bronx on December 18, 1961. Various senders were visited and in each case the senders claimed they had found the stamps in small quantities in the streets. None were aware that the stamps were not genuine.

On January 2, 1962, it was learned that the following lots of counterfeit 4-cent stamps were found in the Bronx:

12/20- 2300 found in vicinity of 1554 Metropolitan Ave, Bronx 62

12/20 –1200 found in Woolworth Store, 1488 Metropolitan Ave., Bronx 62

12/20-187 found near Archer Ave & Beach Ave, Bronx 60

12/20- 700 found on floor of Chester Bowling Lanes, 1380 Metropolitan Ave. Bronx 62

12/20-200 found on floor of Chester Home, 1380 Metropolitan Ave.

12/22-300 found in basement of 1470 Parkchester Road, Bronx 62

12/23-100 turned over to Carrier Jack Siegel, Bronx 55, by employee of Hunt's Point Supply, 917 Southern Blvd., Bronx 55, N.Y.

These stamps are with the file together with the memorandums from the respective Station Superintendents advising the names and addresses of the patrons who turned them in. Agent Motto was advised of these finds on January 2, 1962.

Approximately 128 pieces of mail bearing counterfeit 4-cent stamps, and removed from the mails at Bronx Central Station, were forwarded to Postal Inspector W.S. Palmer on February 9, 1962 together with the report dated Nov. 22, 1961 from Postal Inspector Fagan and Kallies regarding a possible dealer in counterfeit stamps.

Your attention is invited to the report dated January 5, 1962 from Postal Inspector D.E. Myers. Submitted with that report is one envelope bearing a counterfeit 4-cent stamp and the return address of Carmen Torres, 859 Bruckner Blvd., Bronx N.Y.

This report is submitted to show the status of this investigation. It is noted that since the original find of approximately 4,500 counterfeit 4-cent stamps in Long Island City, N.Y., no other finds in Queens County have been reported. It is believed that this case should be given further attention in Bronx County where the other finds have been made and that Mr. Philip Guarino be re-interviewed in connection with his using fictitious and non-existent addresses when mailing the counterfeit stamps as donations. Attention invited to the fact that two separate finds were made at 1380 Metropolitan Avenue on the same date and also two finds were made by two employees of Hunt's Point Supply Company.

A.G. Davis
Postal Inspector

The aforementioned case report represents a bird's-eye view of some of the investigative steps and presorting procedures that to this day are followed when inspectors begin the tedious job of trying to run down leads in counterfeit stamp cases. When you start with the identification of counterfeits in the mail, this begins a long investigative process. You have to interview the mailers so hopefully you can work your way back to the source of the stamps. Basically, what you are doing is following the bread crumbs back to the sellers/distributors and then hopefully even to the printing press.

Now, to get back to the men who had been arrested in Philadelphia. After the arrest and arraignment of the three defendants, their attorneys had a get together. It appears originally there had been an agreement that Costello and Noce would plead guilty to possession with intent to sell, and that Troiano, purportedly an innocent bystander, would be cut out of the entire thing.

Calling Troiano an innocent bystander is pushing the envelope. His claim was that he had just come along for the ride. He professed his innocence to any criminal activity. He had not printed the stamps, and he had not been trying to sell these stamps. Besides his not understanding how the criminal justice system works, he had another problem. Costello and Noce changed their minds. Another way to look at this: If you are a criminal, or someone who associates with criminals, it is a really good idea to have someone you can give up to the authorities.

One can only imagine Troiano's surprise when he discovered that his buddies were now identifying him as the master counterfeiter and the person who was behind this entire criminal enterprise. The government was playing its usual game of let's make a deal. It is my contention the wrong people were getting the deal, and the real criminals would get to walk off so that a criminal case could be made against Troiano, who had been only peripherally involved. Fortunately for the public record, Troiano refused to play along with what the government wanted.

On June 14, 1965, the government's case against Peter Joseph Troiano was called up in the federal court for the Eastern District of Pennsylvania. Troiano was represented by Frances Kahn, a New York criminal attorney. The first move she made was an attempt to exclude any evidence that the government had seized. Her contention was that the government had arrested her client without either a search or arrest warrant. This is pretty much a pro forma defense motion that is made in just about any criminal trial, and it was destined for failure.

The judge ruled that no arrest warrant was necessary as Troiano was apprehended during the commission of a crime – the possession and the attempted sale of counterfeit stamps. On the seizure of counterfeit stamps without a warrant, the same reasoning was employed. The stamps were seized in a typical buy/bust operation and again a warrant was not necessary. Troiano's attorney would again argue these points in the course of the trial.

In the pre-trial hearing, the government had to explain what happened. It was acknowledged that an informant had been used to set up a meeting so agents could purchase counterfeit stamps. Special Agent Motto had been brought down from New York City to assist, if not to direct the case. He and a local agent would meet with the suspects and negotiate the purchase of the counterfeit stamps. As many as eight agents and postal inspectors would take part in the stake out and subsequent arrests. The problem the government faced was establishing that Troiano was knowingly playing a part in what was occurring. On the surface, the only thing the government had on Troiano was that he was behind the wheel of the car that had the stamps in the trunk.

This vehicle did not belong to Troiano. The registered owner was a relative of the other two individuals who had been arrested. Another problem discovered, there was a minor conflict in the statements as to where Troiano actually was when arrested. Was he arrested when he approached the car, entering the car, or when actually trying to start the car? The biggest problem was that at no point could Troiano be directly connected to or involved in the negotiations for the sale of the counterfeit stamps.

It was Miss Kahn's contention that "under the circumstances of this case the only thing the agents could have done in this situation was to question him (Troiano) or detain him for questioning, but they could not arrest him on the mere grounds that he had entered the car, or he was about to enter the car, whether it contained contraband or not." The judge did not agree. He ruled that both the seizure of the stamps and the arrest were legitimate and the stamps would not be excluded as evidence.

After the judge made this ruling, he immediately moved to pick a jury and go to trial. That is when Miss Kahn threw a curve ball I did not expect. She said:

> We would like to waive a jury trial in this case. I have discussed it with my client and he agrees with me, and the United States Attorney has no objection.
>
> We feel that this case will resolve itself on a matter of law and that the issue that could be decided – the question of guilt or innocence could be just as well decided by your honor.

I no longer remember where or when I first heard this, but time and again I have heard the admonishment: "If you are guilty, ask for a jury. If you are innocent, ask for the judge."

The Trial

J. Shane Creamer, the First Assistant United States Attorney laid out the government's case:

> On July 9th of 1962, defendants Costello and Noce entered nolo contendere pleas, I believe before Your Honor, and they have been sentenced to I think five years probation each.
>
> Subsequently, on January 31, 1964, this criminal indictment was brought by the Federal Grand Jury here in the Eastern District of Pennsylvania, and I am referring to Criminal No. 21627, which is the case that is about to be tried and it is a one-count indictment against this defendant, Peter Joseph Troiano, charging that on or about October 10th, 1961 defendant Troiano did knowingly and unlawfully possess with the intent to sell approximately a million counterfeit four-cent stamps, so it is the government's position that after Your Honor has heard the testimony in this case that you will find Peter Joseph Troiano did possess, knowingly with the intent to sell, these million counterfeit stamps.

The first witness called was Joseph Costello. He testified that both he and his uncle had met Peter Troiano just a few weeks before they were arrested. In his rendition it was Troiano who was trying to get their help in delivering some merchandise to Philadelphia. To make the delivery they would use two automobiles. Costello borrowed a car from Charles Fillippo, and this car was dropped off with Troiano, who a few hours later joined them at another location. The two vehicles were then driven to Philadelphia, with Troiano in one car, and Costello and Noce in another. According to Costello, they had no idea what it was Troiano was transporting.

Costello testified it was not until they had checked into the hotel that he and his uncle reportedly learned that the merchandise transported was stamps. At one time or another as many as five people would be in the hotel room they had rented when the sale of stamps was being discussed. Two of those men would be government informants. The government would call neither of these men to substantiate Costello's statement. Then when it came time for serious negotiation to take place, it was Costello who would go up to the 12th floor, not Troiano. This is Costello, the person who prior to his arrival at the hotel had no knowledge of the counterfeit stamps. Does anyone other than myself see that just possibly there is a problem with this person's testimony?

When it was Miss Kahn's turn to cross-examine Costello, she tore into him. It started with the standard questions of any government witness who had also been arrested, and then suddenly became the prosecution's "best friend." "Mr. Costello, you pled guilty to these charges, have you not?" He acknowledged that he had been arrested, sentenced and then placed on probation. Asked if his sentence was the result of his cooperation with the government, he gave the standard response that no promises had been made.

Glaring holes in Costello's testimony occurred when he talked about the buyers examining the stamps. He was pinned down about when he first saw a sample of the stamps that were being shown to the prospective buyer.

> Q: Were any stamps displayed at that time to the buyers before they actually went out to the car? (Here he tried to avoid an answer but eventually he was pinned down).
>
> Q: Had any of these stamps been displayed in front of you?
>
> A: They had a sample.
>
> Q: Did you take the sample upstairs?

A: I don't recall. I don't recall.

Q: When for the first time did you see the stamps?

A: When did I see the stamps? When we were arrested they put them in front of me.

Right from the get go here, first with the testimony of Costello and later with the testimony of Noce there are significant problems. I do not know what the legal standard was in 1960, but it is my strong suspicion that an attorney or U.S. Attorney today who knowingly let his witness perjurer himself would be subject to disbarment. That perjury was occurring here should be obvious to everyone.

Costello would be forced back to what he claimed was the first time he saw the stamps. Finally he acknowledged there already was a sheet of stamps in the agent's possession up in the room on the 12th floor. One problem this represented for the prosecution of Troiano was that the only person who was going back and forth between the 3rd and the 12th floor rooms where the negotiations took place was Costello and one of the government's agents. Testimony would suggest that Costello had been in contact with agents for some time. Troiano never left the third-floor room nor did he take part in any negotiations. Then there was a telling question: "Did you ever at any time actually see Mr. Troiano in possession of any of these stamps?"

A: I don't recall because – I don't recall exactly where these stamps were, the sheet of stamps, up or down.

Q: Did you ever see Peter Troiano in possession of any of those boxes?

A: No.

To impeach Costello's testimony, Miss Kahn made a motion that the United States Attorney produce the testimony given by this witness before the grand jury as well as any statements that he might have made to the agents or reports relative to his conduct that the agents might have noted.

I really do not understand the request for grand jury testimony. To the best of my knowledge testimony given before a grand jury is not released and this would be no exception. The judge was not about to surrender grand jury testimony to Ms. Kahn; however, he must have had his own questions. He relented to the point that he would review the transcript himself. Any reports of the agents were another story. He ruled that any statements or government reports in this case be turned over to the defense. The only thing produced was a three-page statement dated July 10, 1962, which coincided with Costello's plea with the government.[15]

It was at this point that the prosecutor produced another little nugget that went something like this: "Your Honor, the government also possesses two tapes that I would like to speak with you about. There is also a complete recording, also a little indistinct in parts, of the upper room, 1221."

If there were not enough questions already with this prosecution, some major legal issues would be presented with the handling of electronic surveillance. First, the defense had not been informed that these recordings existed until just before the trial commenced. Technically the defense should have filed for disclosure of any electronic surveillance in pre-trial. Second, no attempt had been made by the government to transcribe what was on the tapes. As there were no transcripts provided to the judge, or the defense, these conversations and the negotiations recorded were not available to impeach the questionable testimony of witnesses.[16] All of this should have been done long before the trial even began. These tape recordings would be a point of major confrontation throughout the trial, and in subsequent legal action.

The next witness called was Vincent Noce. He described how he had met Troiano and introduced him to Mr. Costello, who was his nephew. He told how they planned to make a trip to Philadelphia, and how they had to acquire a vehicle for Mr. Troiano. Then he testified about what occurred in the third-floor hotel room:

> Q: Who was in the hotel room?
> A: It was Mr. Troiano, Mr. Costello, myself, and I believe it was a Mr. Martin and then Blaney.
> Q: All right. Were there any conversations while you were in that

15 It is not by accident that frequently miscellaneous case notes are shredded after you do your case reports. Cannot speak for other agencies, but inspectors never turned over case reports.

16 In the context of today's courts, the way the electronic surveillance was handled by the government would automatically be grounds for a mistrial or reversible error.

room relating to stamps?

A: Yes.

Q: Can you state whether or not Mr. Troiano participated in the conversation about the stamps?

A: Oh, yes.

Q: And what was the conversation concerning the stamps?

A: Well, he told Martin that he had the stamps and – I think Martin made a phone call – he didn't mention stamps on the phone, he says he is here with the stuff, and a while later on Blaney called him.

Q: Was there further conversation as to price?

A: Well, I believe that the price was established between Troiano and Martin.

Noce's testimony was most damaging, and probably fixed in the mind of the judge that Mr. Troiano had been actively involved in the attempted sale of counterfeit stamps. If Vincent Noce's testimony was credible, it established that Troiano was not only knowingly involved with these stamps, but most likely could have been the driving force behind the attempted sale, if not the entire criminal enterprise.

Agent Carmine J. Motto was called as a witness and laid out his impressive credentials. Before he became an agent he served as a Marine in the Pacific in World War Two. Discharged, he went into the New York State Police, and then the Secret Service. He described how he had been an agent in the Secret Service for 24 years. Stationed in New York City, he had worked on a number of counterfeit stamp cases.[17] "Throughout the years I have been asked – I have been called upon to look at stamps and judge whether they were counterfeit, on many occasions." Called in to assist in this case, he was the agent who had examined these items and identified them as counterfeit.

Q: Would you indicate what you based your judgment on?

A: First of all, the stamps are printed on a glossy paper, which the government does not use. It is a pre-gummed paper. The government gums the paper after printing. There are many

17 Once again we are presented with a quandary. What were these counterfeit stamp cases between 1949 and 1961? There is a big hole in the public record here, and oh I so wish he would have talked more about this in his book.

defects in the portrait on the stamp. The holes around the stamps, the perforations are not the same as the government uses; that is the different widths in the size of the holes. Any of these reasons would make the stamp counterfeit.

The stamps were offered and then placed into evidence. The judge was clearly interested in the testimony of Agent Motto and began to ask him his own questions.

Q: Mr. Motto, what are the defects that you say existed in the portrait?
A: There are little marks on the portrait here. These little spots that I see would show a defect in the plate. Much of the work around the hair is missing. If you look here you have a big white spot here that does not appear quite as white here. There is over-all softness. If you run your finger over the stamps you can feel the engraving. That is from the steel plate. This is photoengraving. This is smooth.
Q: Now I also direct your attention to the plate number. I imagine that is what it is called, on each of these stamps (sheets). Did you notice anything about them as far as (the exhibit) is concerned. They are all the ... , aren't they?
A: These are all – the plate number on the counterfeit stamps is the same.
Q: These have 26401, all of them; is that right?
A: Yes.

When reading a trial transcript it is a real treat to find such clear and concise testimony from a witness. Agent Motto had given an excellent description of how he had, and how anyone else could easily identify that the items in question were in fact counterfeit, and not made by the government.

Motto would go on to describe how in the course of the negotiations Costello had given him the keys to the car used to transport the stamps. The purpose was so the undercover agent could verify both the quantity and quality of the stamps that had been transported to Philadelphia for sale. In Motto's testimony he then went on to describe how he had taken the stamps to the Secret Service office, verified they were counterfeit and again parked the car outside the hotel.

Motto returned to room 1221 and had an extensive conversation with Agent Deckard, the other undercover officer involved in the negotiations. Still trying to get the other parties involved in the negotiations, Motto advised Deckard not to buy the stamps. Quite an argument ensued with Costello for the next hour or so. Costello kept trying to have the sale go through and Motto was saying no.

While all of these negotiations were going on, Costello reportedly was consulting with his codefendants down in room 343. This was both by phone and by going back and forth between the rooms. It never was established in any testimony that Peter Troiano took part in any of these conversations. Apparently he spent his time dozing on one of the beds.

The bargaining began at $20,000 and when Motto complained about the quality of both the perforations and the printing, eventually Costello was forced down substantially. Costello argued that they had already made changes both to the quality of the perforations and printing. They apparently had put a plate number on the sheets at the request of an undercover agent. Still Motto would not accept the deal. In frustration, early in the morning the would-be stamp sellers walked out of the hotel with the announced intention of returning to New York. When they went to their vehicles they were arrested.

The first day's proceedings ended at 3:20 and the court adjourned until the next morning. It was only at this point that the prosecutor turned over to the defense the raw tape recordings for review. Miss Kahn would spend the night trying to listen to and decipher who was saying what to whom.

The import of the tape recording controversy cannot be stressed enough for the ultimate impact it would have on the legal proceedings. Most likely the government had looked upon the prosecution of Troiano as a done deal and not a lot of forethought or preparation had gone on with the trial. No notice was given to the defense that the tape recordings existed. Then in the almost four years before the trial commenced, no effort had been made to either clean up or transcribe these recordings.

When the next day the defense would try to use the tape

recording, Judge Lord would state that he had no desire to sit through hours of scrambled recordings. This would seriously hamper Ms. Kahn in her efforts to impeach the witnesses in cross-examination. Still, she tried. Under cross-examination of Costello, the following occurred:

> Q: Did you know who manufactured them (the stamps) or who printed them?
>
> A: No.
>
> Q: Did you know how they were manufactured or how they were printed?
>
> A: No.

Additional testimony would demonstrate that Costello had just perjured himself.

From reading the trial transcript it is suspected that most likely Judge Lord had not had to deal with electronic surveillance before. Remember this was still the dark ages in the utilization of this technology and firm judicial guidelines were just beginning to come down from higher courts. The defense's efforts were not exactly helped by the prosecution either. Every attempt that Ms. Kahn would make to use the tapes or have them transcribed would be obstructed. Most likely this was not an accident. From the bits and pieces that Ms. Kahn was able to get into evidence, it was evident that what was on the tapes directly contradicted the testimony of both Costello and Noce. The prosecutor would argue that none of this mattered as Troiano was being charged with possession with the intent to sell. "We are not here dealing with a charge of selling."

Kahn argued the only connection the government could establish between Troiano and the bogus stamps was that at one point or another he had been in the car used for transporting the stamps. This was the heart of her defense. There was no evidence showing that Troiano had anything to do with manufacturing the stamps, selling the stamps, or that he had any knowledge about the production of stamps. The same could not be said for Costello. Kahn read into the transcript conversations Costello had with the undercover agents in which he showed an intimate knowledge about counterfeit stamp production. On the tape recordings he directly contradicts his testimony that he knew nothing about the stamps in this case:

> Miss Kahn: Mr. Costello – he says there is 200,000 in a package, there is 100,000 in each wrapper, two wrappers in a box, five boxes. There is an argument about the fact there is no tissue between them. He tells the men that you don't need tissue. He goes into the manufacture of how it is made. He talks about the presses, how he will run them all day and he will print as many as they need. He also in this conversation on the tape refers to counterfeit money that he has at home – $10s, $20s, how he – you have got to pick your spot in passing them. During this conversation Costello tells him (the agent) that he wouldn't counterfeit sweepstakes tickets. He tells how he has been dealing with shylocks and all about counterfeiting bonds.

Arguing about the quality of the stamps, Costello commented:

> You wouldn't have sent for us if you didn't think they weren't any good. We sent you the sample; we changed the plate. The perforating machine was imperfect and we even changed the numbers when we ran off some more of them.

He acknowledged that he had sold a batch (group of stamps) before. In another conversation recorded, Agent Deckard had commented that the mastermind behind the whole thing was Noce. (This testimony was excluded by the judge.)

It is fairly obvious what had occurred. The Secret Service had solid cases against Costello and Noce. The case against Troiano was anything but strong. To support a conviction a decision had been made to use the others against him. To get this testimony, the government cut a deal. This happens all too frequently in the criminal justice system and in most cases the end may justify the means. In this case there may just be a question of the ethical standards being applied. A question that maybe the authorities should have asked was to what degree was Troiano really criminally culpable. Was he a criminal or just plain stupid?[18]

18 This question resonates in our current criminal justice system. If you plead guilty we will give you a deal. If you profess your innocence we will lock you away.

The Secret Service had bigger fish to fry than Troiano. Their primary concern was to take down the press that apparently was putting out not only stamps, but also currency and bonds. Costello appeared to be a wealth of information on that subject. It is expected that at least part of their bargain was that the government would seize the plant and plates in New York. This was their highest priority. Troiano was simply collateral damage and demonstrated the danger of hanging out with the wrong people. When Troiano drove the car from New York transporting the counterfeit stamps, he knew what he was doing and was taking active participation in the crime.[19]

The position the court took on Costello's testimony was spelled out: "I must say that I have some difficulty at this moment, except for the impeachment purposes, in seeing the relevance of this because the charge here is a very narrow one; namely, that the defendant was in knowing possession with the intent to sell."

The issue for the judge was limited to Troiano's possession with intent to sell. He had been arrested in the car that had the counterfeit stamps in the trunk. It stands to reason that he knew contraband was in the trunk and that the people he was with were there to sell this contraband. In his ruling Judge Lord cited the 1961 case of Hill v. United States 294 Federal Second 562, an Eight Circuit decision. This case covered an arrest for possession of a sawed-off shotgun that was found in a suitcase in the trunk of a car. The Eight Circuit had held that this constituted possession.

Still, the defense was not going to roll over and play dead. Sentencing occurred on October 5, 1965, and Ms. Kahn promptly lit into the government's case:

> At this time, your honor, I respectfully move to set aside the verdict and dismiss the indictment on the grounds that there was no probable cause to arrest the defendant and the evidence introduced at the trial was illegally seized and should have been suppressed.
>
> Your honor, I further move to set aside the verdict of the Court and move for a new trial upon all the exceptions and objections taken by me during the course of this trial and without limiting the generality of my motion, upon the following exceptions taken by me, to wit.

19 If you drive your buddy to a bank, and he tries to rob the place, even though you never leave the seat of the car, you will be charged as a participant in the robbery. More than one person has gone to prison swearing they had no idea what was going on. This is very common in narcotics cases.

My exception to your Honor's ruling that the defense be permitted to transcribe the tape, which is Exhibit D-2, in evidence, and your Honor's refusing to permit us to have time to have the tape transcribed.

I also move upon your Honor's refusal to rule on my motion as to whether or not I would be permitted to transcribe the tape before I rested my case. At that time I informed the Court that the defendant would take the stand if I was given the opportunity to transcribe this tape. Your Honor's statement that your decision as to whether or not I would be permitted to have the tape transcribed depends on whether or not the defendant took the stand that is on page 195-196 of the record; this actually operated to deprive this defendant of the right to testify in his own behalf and amounted to testimonial compulsion.

I further move to set aside the verdict and for a new trial upon the ground that the verdict is against the evidence and against the weight of the evidence, and that the defendant had not been proven guilty beyond a reasonable doubt.

There was no testimony by any government agent that the defendant participated in the intended sale of counterfeit stamps. The only testimony against the defendant was given by his codefendants, Noce and Costello, who are related to each other and who have every motive to lie.

It is interesting to note that they are both older by many years than the defendant, who at that time was 22 years of age; that they owned and supplied the cars that were involved; that they had guns in their possession; that Costello had dealt personally with Blaney and the agents; that Blaney tells the agents that Noce is the boss; and the coup de grace of the matter is that Noce and Costello are the ones who share in the expense money. (Provided by the Inspection Service)

I therefore renew my motion to set aside the verdict and acquit the defendant.

The response of the judge: Motion's denied.

The judge asked Troiano if he wished to address the court and he replied, "The only thing is that I am innocent of the charges." Some seeds of doubt must have been planted. Judge Lord stated that he required some further information and study about this young man before he would hand down a sentence. Pending his receiving this report, he sentenced Troiano to the maximum – five years to be served. This is a common practice in federal court before a final adjudication.

When you try to research any postal counterfeiting, one of your greatest frustrations is the paucity of a public record available for your review. In this case we are blessed with a defendant who continued to protest his innocence, and had adequate legal representation. The conviction was appealed to the Third Circuit, and argued April 18, 1966. The conviction was sustained, but once again this was not the end of the road.

Notice was filed that the defendant intended to file a petition for a writ of certiorari to the United States Supreme Court. On November 21, 1966 the Supreme Court denied the petition and the case was returned to the District Court. On the surface it would appear that the government had prevailed here, but it is apparent that Troiano's insistence on his innocence was giving Judge Lord pause. On June 15, 1967, the original sentence of five years' imprisonment was reduced to three, which in turn was suspended. The judge did, however, impose a fine of $1,000.

The prosecutor made an interesting statement to the judge:

> The Secret Service agents who investigated this case investigated not only this attempted sale of a million counterfeit four-cent stamps but thoroughly investigated, traced back the source of how these stamps were prepared, where the paper was purchased, where the stamps were, in effect made. (This was part of the deal with Costello and Noce.)
>
> Their investigations were frustrated, but they have been able to ascertain that this was a highly organized, well-organized group of individuals who prepared, manufactured and delivered these stamps for sale. (Can one say, organized crime? Stating that the investigation was frustrated indicates that Costello and Noce double crossed the Secret Service and never followed through on their part in the deal.)

Miss Kahn had a few caustic comments to make of her own:

> I personally know of one instance in which a man had gone to the agents; I don't know whether to the agents here in Philadelphia, but he has gone to the agents in New York, and informed them of the fact that it was not Troiano who started this organization, but that it was in fact Noce and Costello, so that I don't know what the agents – and this is a Secret Service

agent in New York. His name is Mr. Wong.

I don't know if you know Mr. Wong, if you have been in contact with him, but I know that he knows.

I don't know if he did any investigation of it but I know there is somebody that told him that long before this that he was offered these stamps by Noce and Costello, and not by Troiano, and that Troiano had nothing to do with it.

As stated previously an unknown number of these 4-cent Lincoln counterfeits did get out in the market. They had been on sale at a number of locations in the New York City area. Periodically, they will show up in philatelic auctions or in the stock books of stamp dealers. Cancelled items usually bear the postmark of Grand Central Station.

A History Lesson

Counterfeiting is primarily the domain of the Secret Service so when reviewing just about any counterfeiting case it is not unusual to find their agents prominently involved. Today when we think of the Secret Service our first thought is of the brave men and women who without hesitation put their lives in danger to protect those we put into executive office. The history of the service was not always so positive, or for that matter legitimate. It has long been forgotten that this was a law enforcement agency that was created out of thin air. It was founded with neither presidential nor congressional authorization. A Government official simply did it on his own.

It is commonly not remembered that before the Civil War there was no official U.S. paper currency. The Constitution only authorizes the government to issue coins, not fiat currency. The paper currency that was in circulation was issued by about 250 private banks scattered through the states. One would be hard pressed to design a system more open to abuse and fraud if one deliberately tried. It should not come as a surprise to discover that by the 1860s it is estimated at least 80 percent of the paper currency in circulation was counterfeit.

In the closing days of the Civil War a bureaucrat in the Treasury Department with neither congressional nor executive authorization decided this was a problem that needed to be remedied. On his own he began to recruit individuals whose job it would be to combat counterfeiting.[20] He figured that the best way to catch a thief was to hire a thief. About 50 percent of the original agents hired were themselves known counterfeiters. Not surprisingly, a number of these individuals would fall back into old habits. In its infancy, the reputation this generated for the fledgling agency suffered for many years as a result.

Surviving political infighting, the Secret Service was officially recognized and sanctioned. Under the administration of President Grant it began the transformation into the professional organization it is today. In 1874 Elmer Washburn began the transformation: "Employees will be judged by the character they sustain, by the results they accomplish, and by the manner in which they accomplish them."

Year by year, and case by case, the reputation for professionalism would grow. With the turn of the last century and the assassination of a President by a disgruntled office seeker they would take over the duty for protection. Still, they would never forget their first responsibility, the protection of the nation's currency. By statute postage stamps were defined as an obligation of the government, and as such, they also were considered to be under the purview of the Secret Service.

Thanks primarily to the Great Depression and World War II, the public began to buy into the concept of "Federal Government." As the agents of the Secret Service and other investigative agencies became more professional, their reputation for honesty and integrity would be recognized by both the public in general and the court system in particular. Today, when an agent raises his hand in court, be they Secret Service, Postal or U.S. Marshall, that testimony is generally accepted as gospel. It is a public trust which has been earned gradually and which historically has been well justified.

20 "A Nation of Counterfeiters," Stephen Mihm, Harvard University Press, 2007

3

All Hell Breaks Loose

Detroit 1967

Over the years different individuals have mentioned to me that the 5-cent Washington stamp had been counterfeited. I had never seen a copy of this stamp or any official reports of an investigation. Then one day I did find a reference that demonstrated this stamp really had been duplicated. When I was looking at a listing of old Inspection Service cases I found case number 109157-MD for Detroit, Michigan. The only notes in the file provided little information.

> Arrested Michael Thomas, Michael Lazarov, Andrew Asaro, and Joseph Yopollo for counterfeiting of currency. Incident to this arrest, a quantity of counterfeit stamps and the plate for printing 5-cent stamps were discovered.

That was it. Nada, zip, no additional information. Saving the day, when I dug further, I discovered there had been a trial. If it had not been for the trial record, once again another case would have disappeared into the fog of time. When I reviewed the transcript I soon concluded most likely the Secret Service would have wished the court documents had disappeared.

This story actually begins in Chicago sometime in 1964. Apparently the Secret Service had zeroed in on Michael Thomas and Michael Lazarov as individuals who were involved in counterfeiting activity. Reading between the lines of the little public record available, I suspected this activity actually was with postage stamps.[21] Suddenly, in the fall of 1967, Thomas and Lazarov packed up and moved first to Royal Oak, and then Detroit, Michigan. It appears that a Secret Service surveillance team moved with them. Somehow agents were keeping track of what these men were doing, and it was the agents' belief that a new counterfeiting operation was in the works.

---

21 Years later a conversation I had with a counterfeiter would suggest this was true.

By paging through court documents, one is able to piece together the chain of events. One of the first items found was a motion the defense filed to suppress any evidence seized by the government. This is pretty much a pro forma motion for just about every defense attorney. In this case it apparently had merit. In the affidavit the defense contended that a search had occurred that was not supported by benefit of a warrant. The defense claimed the search that took place was illegal, and any evidence the government seized should be thrown out and not considered by the court. To justify their action, the government was forced to respond. Ronald V. Germaine, then a special agent with the United States Secret Service, filed the papers. In doing so, an extensive part of the government's investigation had to be exposed.

Germaine described how on November 21, 1967, he filed a criminal complaint charging Michael Lazarov with a violation of Title 18, U.S.C.A., Section 501 (stamp counterfeiting). Based on his complaint an arrest warrant had been issued for Lazarov's arrest. Then, instead of affecting this arrest, Germaine put both Lazarov and a garage he was using on Woodward Street in Detroit under surveillance. Germaine never came out and acknowledged this, but his agents were stalling. They identified four individuals as involved in a counterfeiting operation but still they waited. The excuse given was they wanted to have all four men in the building when they pounced. Not stated was that they wanted to be sure the individuals they were watching had actually begun the production of counterfeits before the government moved in.

Finally on December 5, after many days of 24-hour surveillance, Agent Germaine apparently concluded enough time had gone by. He gave the word to move in. Still, one of their suspects, Asaro, had wandered off. With guns drawn, Germaine and another agent hit the side door of the garage, and immediately confronted Michael Thomas and Joseph Yopollo. Germaine informed the two men they were under arrest, and he then went room by room searching for Lazarov. He was found hiding in a back room.

Germaine testified that when he found Lazarov, there "in plain sight," lying on the floor near him, were the back impressions of $20 dollar Federal Reserve notes. Brought together, the three men were advised of their constitutional rights. It was about this time that the fourth suspect, Asaro, came wandering back into the building carrying two bottles of a printing sensitizer.

Now, with four men in handcuffs and agents already in the building, the U.S. attorney was called and belatedly a search warrant was obtained for the building. Once it was issued, a complete search was conducted, and extensive evidence seized. A cynical person might conclude that the delay in arresting Lazarov had been deliberate. This man could have been taken into custody on many occasions prior to the date of his arrest. The excuse the agent gave was they wanted to get all four members of the gang together in the building before they moved. Then, if the men could be grabbed in the building, this would have the added benefit of providing the agents the opportunity to look around.

The prosecutor would argue that the agents had simply been executing the arrest warrant they had for Michael Lazarov. They knew he was in the building, and had to search this structure to find the suspect. When he was found, he was hiding in a back room, and there in plain sight was contraband. It was the partially completed Federal Reserve notes. The U.S. Attorney would also profess that Yopollo and Thomas really had not been officially arrested until after Lazarov had been taken into custody.[22]

Not surprisingly, it was the position of the government that the complaint upon which the original arrest warrant was issued was valid, the arrest was proper, and probable cause submitted to a Federal District Judge had been proper and sufficient for the search warrant to be issued. "To hold that the government cannot arrest a defendant while in the act with others, of committing a crime is absurd."

The government had a couple of problems to overcome here. The first was they had the arrest warrant for Lazarov for about a month, and they had been watching him come and go. He could have been grabbed on many occasions prior to his being picked up. Then secondly, they had searched the facility without a warrant. They justified this search by sighting the case of United States v. Rabinowitz 339 U.S. 56 (1950). This was quoted as the prevailing constitutional

22 If you do not have freedom to come and go, you are under arrest. When an agent has a gun pointed at your nose, I doubt if that would be defined as having freedom of movement.

pronouncement in the area of what constitutes the permissible scope of a search when it occurs incident to a lawful arrest. Rabinowitz has come to stand for the proposition that incident to a lawful arrest, the immediate area that is under the "control" of the person arrested is fair game for search without a warrant.

It is only fitting that Rabinowitz would be cited as justification for a search in a case involving postage stamps. Rabinowitz had been a major East Coast stamp dealer in New York City. One day his business was visited by a postal inspector investigating a complaint of counterfeit overprints being printed on legitimate United States postage stamps. With the overprinting the collector value would be enhanced. When the inspector entered Rabinowitz's showroom the first thing he saw was a printing press that he believed was used for the overprinting. Considering this a big clue, the inspector went on to arrest Rabinowitz and then search the business, and found the evidence used to convict him. A point that should be considered by any stamp collector – when you see a printing press or other tools used to alter the state or condition of collections stamps in your favorite stamp dealer's office, just maybe it is time to look for another stamp dealer.[23]

On January 23, 1968, a five-count indictment was returned in this case. This was a Secret Service investigation so it should not come as any surprise that four of the five criminal counts related to the counterfeiting of currency. It was only in the fifth count it was charged the four defendants did possess with intent to use one counterfeit five-cent postage stamp aluminum offset printing plate, a violation of Section 501. Then almost as an afterthought a sixth count was added that charged the defendants with conspiracy.

If the government believed this case would simply slide through the system, that delusion disappeared on June 25, when the attorney who represented Asaro filed a motion to suppress, and for the return of any and all evidence that had been seized illegally by the agents. The following grounds were enumerated:

1. That Andrew Asaro was arrested while on property belonging to another over which he had no ownership or control. That there was no pre-existing

23 Another noted New York stamp dealer had a printing press in his show room. That was S.A. Taylor who at the turn of the last century was producing more stamp varieties than many countries.

warrant for his arrest, and there was nothing that supported the charge of possession that was lodged against him.

2. Evidence on the property was illegally seized as the Secret Service had seized this material prior to their obtaining a search warrant.

3. Entry of the Secret Service agents on the property was illegal and was based on an invalid arrest warrant.

4. The defendant makes the motion to suppress on the basis that his arrest and the search were both unlawful. That the search was not incident to a valid arrest, and that the arrest was made for the purposes of a search, and thus the evidence seized should be suppressed. An arrest must stand on its own, and it cannot subsequently be made good by what a subsequent search may turn up.

November 8, 1968, was not a good day in Detroit for either the U.S. Attorney or the Secret Service. The judge who was hearing this case decided the motion filed by the defense had merit, and he found for the defendant. With this ruling all the evidence seized was automatically inadmissible, and the entire case was dismissed.

The U.S. Attorney promptly filed a new criminal case against Thomas and Yopollo. This time the Secret Service decided they would use a secret weapon. It appeared they had recruited Lazarov to appear as a government witness. This must have been a movement out of desperation as in return they were giving Lazarov a pass on any of his open charges. This should strike the average observer as strange. Lazarov did have an extensive criminal record with such minor offenses as armed robbery and felonious assault. At the time this trial would take place he still had five open criminal cases against him (one of which was for counterfeiting stamps) that now mysteriously would disappear.[24]

When the second trial commenced, the first witness the defense tried to call was Asaro. The Secret Service was not really happy about this, and before Asaro could take the stand and testify, an agent in the hallway took him aside and had a few words. In no uncertain terms

24Now this is conjecture, but what if Lazarov had been turned as a government informant way back when he was in Chicago? Could this have caused the time delay in executing the raid? Could the delay have been because they were waiting for Lazarov to tell them they had finally produced counterfeits? Then when agents did move in they just happened to find Lazarov next to the evidence they would need. Just a thought.

Asaro was told that if he testified, he would again be prosecuted. He was informed the government would find something to charge him with, and they would do everything they could to send him to prison. Now, if you are going to threaten a defense witness like this, it probably is a really good idea that you not do this where it can be overheard by one of the defense attorneys. I have not made this up. It happened.

Having been personally threatened by a Secret Service agent, it should not surprise anyone that Asaro suddenly decided to disappear. The trial did go on, and with the primary defense witness now missing, Yopollo and Thomas were convicted. Their attorneys promptly filed appeals. In this round of appeals the same problems were there for the prosecution as had existed in the first case. Added to that was the new wrinkle of what happened in the hall that caused the defense's star witness to decide he wanted to disappear. When the Sixth Circuit Court discovered what had happened they let the government know they were not happy, and once again this case was tossed. The Secret Service still did not get the message. They promptly walked down the hall and tried to sell their case to the Organized Crime Strike Force.

The argument the Secret Service would make to the Strike Force attorneys was that the plate to make the counterfeit stamps had been contracted for by organized crime in Chicago.[25] Asked to identify what the connection was to organized crime, they pointed to their new best buddy – Lazarov. He owned the building that was being used for the counterfeit operation. Before that he had been using it for the production of pornographic movies. At that time, organized crime controlled the production and distribution of about 90 percent of the porn business in the United States.

Most likely the Strike Force attorneys were not really thrilled with the case the Secret Service was belatedly dumping in their laps. Still they were not just blown off. At the same time they were not really killing themselves to bring this case to court either. There would be a slight delay before the government would go after Thomas again – like 800 days. By now I would guess that just about every level of the federal court system was more than a little upset with both the Justice

25 It is my suspicion that the 5-cent Washington counterfeit originated with individuals I would get to know in Chicago. More on that later.

Department and the Secret Service. This time the court would inform the government that – ah, you guys do know about this little thing called speedy trial?

Finally, the Secret Service and the U.S. Attorney got the hint and this case died. One currency operation appears to have been broken up. Oh, and one set of plates to print stamps had also been found. Nobody went to jail. Then I had a personal connection to this story. One day I was sitting at my desk in Chicago and the phone rang. After the caller determined who I was, the salutation from this individual was "Hi, I'm the guy who made the plates for the 5-cent Washington." He described how he did contract work for the "Mob." He claimed that when they needed a counterfeiting operation set up, he was the guy they would call. Detroit was a spin off from an organized crime case in Chicago. I would meet some of the other local players as they would again be involved in some of my own investigations.

Once again it needs to be said that when I relate these stories this is not meant as an attack on the agents involved. All I can say is sometimes you win, sometimes you lose. Sometimes when you are pushing the envelope you make mistakes and the courts slap you down. As a field agent you try to make the best decisions you can, and sometimes you are just flat wrong. That is why we have defense attorneys. It is probably because of these mistakes that we know most of what we do about stamp counterfeiting or any other criminal activity for that matter. If someone simply goes into court and pleads guilty, little if any public record is generated.

New York, New York 1968

The below was written before John Hotchner shared the postal counterfeit stamp display he had put together with Richard Drews and Joann Lenz. One item displayed was a mailing envelope sent to a well-known Boston stamp dealer postmarked May 1970. The stamp on the envelope was the 6-cent Franklin D. Roosevelt that may have originated from this case. If so, obviously neither the Secret Service nor the postal inspectors had seized all the stamps produced. It should be noted that nobody is going to simply print 1,000 sheets of counterfeit stamps and then walk away.

> 97052-MD March 1968 – Ronald Fletcher, who was a known printer of counterfeit money, delivered to the Secret Service 1,000 sheets of 6-cent Roosevelt stamps (Scott #1305). On March 7, the Secret Service picked up Fletcher, William Nelson, and John Louis Alves.
>
> No additional counterfeit stamps are known to have been seized. It is not known if the plates or press that produced the bogus items were ever located. The Secret Service reported they believed that after a single printing the plates and other evidence related to this case had then been destroyed by burning. No other information is known.

In Hotchner's display, the stamp is described as lithographed and not a bad reproduction. It was perforated 12.5 on each side compared to the genuine article that is perforated 10.5 X 11. The item displayed by Hotchner even had the electric eye bars on the bottom of the stamp, although they were not of the proper size. This is a stamp to look for in mixtures as it is generally unknown in collector circles. It must also be noted that this was not the only time this particular stamp issue has been copied, but the details of the other endeavors are not known.

Reidville, Georgia 1969

A stretch in the penitentiary can be a life-changing experience. For many it can also be a vocational training program. More than one counterfeiter has either learned or honed his skill while a guest of the government. In 1969, two men in the maximum-security facility located at Reidville, Georgia really worked at developing their job skills. While working in the prison printing shop, they gained stature with their fellow inmates by taking care of inmate postage needs. Everything was going just fine until the local postmaster in this small Georgia town concluded one day that something just did not look right with some of the 6-cent stamps he was observing on letters coming out of the local institution. At the same time the Secret Service was trying to identify who in the prison had produced several thousand dollars in bogus $20 bills. Think there might be a connection?

Considering the government had a captive audience, it is presumed this situation was eventually resolved in the government's favor.

Turning over a Rock

In the late 1960s, the U.S. Post Office had to again recognize it had a crime problem. Within the Inspection Service, historically there has always been an identity crisis. Were we criminal investigators, or were we auditors? Considering themselves glorified accountants, many inspectors did not even bother to carry their issued firearms. Forced to qualify twice a year, a joke frequently heard on the firing line was who had the .38-caliber pencil. Then the Plymouth mail robbery occurred. This was the largest robbery in American history. The investigation that followed was a comedy of errors. Then in Chicago there was another incident. Two special investigators were killed by a mail thief they failed to properly search and control.

Things had to change. Already faced with increased armed robberies, employee assaults, the loss of $10 to $20 million each year in stamp stock and money orders to post office burglaries, now suddenly there was an explosion in counterfeiting activity. The first step in addressing these problems was to bring in a new chief inspector. He took as his mandate the recruitment of new inspectors and officially put the emphasis back on criminal investigations. For the investigation of stamp counterfeiting these changes may have been just in time.

New York, New York 1969

In case 136649-MD on May 22, 1969, postal inspectors and Secret Service agents arrested Phil Frimet, Jack Warshaw, Vincent Antoniato and Wilson DelGado for the counterfeiting of 6-cent FDR stamps. A total of 4 million stamps are believed to have been seized by the government. The story the government put out was that none of these items had been distributed before the agents moved in. It was reported that the offenders had destroyed the printing plates after the printing of 4 million stamps.

Neither I, nor to the best of my knowledge anybody else, has really dug into this case. What is known is that the newspapers reported these stamps had not been destined for use in the United States mail. Rather, the reported plan had been to send the stamps overseas. These bogus items were to be used as collateral to secure a loan in some unidentified Far Eastern country. If one is involved with organized crime, this plan may not be as ridiculous as it might seem at first sight. It also would not be the last time such a scheme would surface.

The government reported the stamps being found were only a "fair" representation of the original. One glaring difference was the color was slightly off. The stamps had a grayish-brown shade rather than the deep brown color of the legitimate issue. As one Secret Service agent would describe the stamp, "Despite the fact that they were only a fair reproduction of the original, they were as good as money in the Orient." Maybe this was not the dumb idea I originally thought it was.

This counterfeit stamp had been printed at the Anchor Litho Company in New York City. This business was owned by Phil Frimet. When the last bundle of stamps was delivered to the Jet Bindery for perforations, the agents moved in. Obviously this was another case where the Secret Service had been able to move an informant or undercover agent into the operation. Then a case came along that would grab the attention even of the post office.

Pittsburgh 1969

What happened in Pittsburgh would not follow a simple story line. By the mid 1960s J. Edgar Hoover had been dragged kicking and screaming to finally acknowledge that yes there was such a thing as "organized crime." Up to that point, if one of his agents even had the temerity to mention such a thing, he would soon find himself assigned to Butte, Montana.[26] In the twilight of Hoover's reign, slowly but surely, enterprising agents began to venture into this swamp.

26 Those are not my words. I like Butte, Montana. This was an inside joke in the bureau. In the bureau, to those in headquarters, if you got an assignment to Butte this was considered to be America's version of Siberia.

When agents of the Federal Bureau of Investigation went after "the Mob," one of the first targets picked was the production and distribution of pornography. Whether it was being imported from another country, or was being produced in the United States, this was a business upon which the Mob maintained almost a virtual monopoly. It should not surprise anyone that much of this activity would be centered in New York City with tentacles that stretched across the country. Agents in New York began to identify the East Coast distribution network. One channel of distribution they discovered was traced back to Pittsburgh and a name they soon encountered was Anthony (Rocco) DeRamo. On February 6, 1969, the FBI conducted a series of raids across the country. One of the targets they picked to hit was DeRamo's residence.

This raid was a success. At DeRamo's residence, agents found over 500 pounds of pornographic material along with a few other items. There was a submachine gun, four pistols, $50,000 in counterfeit currency, blank U.S. Savings Bonds, and what agents would describe as burglary tools. Other raids in Brooklyn and Rochester, N.Y., New York City, and Cleveland, Ohio, netted similar results. The FBI promptly ran before the cameras to tell the world what they had accomplished.

It is my suspicion that the first time the Secret Service knew about the counterfeit $20 bills found in DeRamo's residence was when they opened the newspaper the next morning. Historically, the FBI has never been known for playing well with others. With the bureau, the sharing of intelligence has generally been noted as being a one-way street. Now, thanks to the FBI, DeRamo would find himself on the Secret Service radar. Having once been identified as possessing counterfeit currency and suspect bonds, DeRamo would now have a bull's eye on his back.

This attention must have paid off. On April 1, 1970, a grand jury indictment came down that charged Anthony Rocco DeRamo, Steve Robert Cunic, and Robert Joseph Beran with possession and selling of counterfeit postage stamps. The offense in this indictment was identified as occurring between the first day of December, 1969 and continuing to the 25th day of January, 1970. Specifically, these individuals were charged with negotiating and then delivering forged stamps to one Nick Louis Fiorentino (an undercover agent) in New York City.

The total number of counterfeit stamps delivered was not really all that significant. It only totaled 152,400 postage stamps. What should have grabbed the attention of postal officials or anyone else concerned with the revenue of the government was the variety of stamps being offered for sale:

41,300 6-cent Franklin D. Roosevelt

18,100 8-cent U.S. Airmail (Capital)

18,000 15-cent Oliver W. Holmes

18,000 13-cent John F. Kennedy

20,600 30-cent Robert E. Lee

36,400 $1 Patrick Henry

Never before had a counterfeit operation put out such a diverse selection of postage stamps. In this operation, how many stamps had actually been printed is anyone's guess, but obviously this had to be a very large operation. Then in March 1971, an additional $500,000 in counterfeit stamps was discovered.

Very little is known about what actually occurred. The people involved were not talking. All that is known is that one morning bundles of stamps were found outside Pittsburgh dumped along a country road. The authorities had found six large bundles. The suspicion was this was due to the pressure coming down from the Secret Service investigation. In this case the stamps they found duplicated were the $1 Patrick Henry, the 10-cent Jefferson Memorial (Scott#1052), as well as the 10-cent Savings Stamp (Scott #S1).

This is the raw newspaper negative from the Pittsburgh Post-Gazette showing a postal inspector in 1969 inspecting recovered counterfeit stamps. The lines show how this photo was cropped for publication. COURTESY PITTSBURGH POST-GAZETTE

Like so many others, the great frustration in this case, is the absence of much in the way of public records. Other than the sensational original headlines, little news coverage was found. Still, the Secret Service was very heavily involved and it is suspected the Inspection Service was as well. The only information I ever received from individual inspectors was the comment that, yes, we had a counterfeit problem. I knew the inspectors had done something. I was just never able to find out what.

Demonstrating that the inspectors were involved, a very small file was discovered at the Washington Crime Laboratory. Inside was a printing plate for the 10-cent Savings Stamp, the 10-cent Independence Hall and the $1 Patrick Henry. There was also a plate for the 15-cent Oliver Wendell Holmes. All of these printing plates were in a 100-stamp format and had no marginal markings. They all demonstrated signs they had seen heavy usage. Unfortunately, there were no accompanying case reports. When questioned, the lab personnel had no information on how these plates came into their possession.

The reasonable assumption is that Pittsburgh had been the location of the printing plant producing these stamps. This is based not only on the quantity of stamps found abandoned alongside a country road, but also the printing plates that had also been discarded. One might wonder why Pittsburgh? This was a good location for operations for a number of reasons. First and foremost, it was a backwater for organized crime. Connected generally to the Genovese family in New York, most crime in Pittsburgh was actually controlled by the local ward politicians and the police force they controlled. In Pittsburgh, organized crime activity was kept very much under the radar. When the Secret Service began to snoop around, this would have generated a great deal of pressure to close the printing operation down. The local politicians and corrupt cops really did not want a bunch of feds snooping around.

If you believe the government was able to account for all the stamps produced, think again. It is known that before the authorities made their presence known a substantial number of these items had been shipped to other locations. Most likely millions of these stamps were distributed and used in the mail without discovery.

Our friend DeRamo did not go away. In August of 1973, he was picked up again. This time it was for his involvement with the forgery of $106,000 in United States Savings Bonds. The FBI records would also show that DeRamo would maintain ongoing involvement with the production and distribution of pornography. He would be investigated for operating unlicensed massage parlors (prostitution), operating a gambling (show boat) operation and continued involvement with the counterfeiting of Savings Bonds, currency, and stamps. Can you say organized crime? You have got to give the guy credit for being an earner.[27]

Boston 1970

The key to researching postage stamp counterfeiting rests on the shoulders of the 50,000 plus stamp collectors scattered from big cities to small all across the United States. Stories that would be ignored

27 A fact the general public is not aware of: counterfeiting has a higher recidivist rate than heroin addiction.

and fall through the cracks with regular "news" would find print in the philatelic press. It is thanks to the many letters and articles that came from vigilant collectors that a public record was created. In 1970, one such attack would be reported in Boston.

On July 6, 1970, *Linn's Stamp* News reported news from Boston. "U.S. Agents Arrest Two with Fake 'Ike' Stamps." Two men had been arrested by Treasury agents and charged with the possession of 47,232 counterfeit copies of the Eisenhower stamp that was issued on October 14, 1969. This was the jumbo stamp, Scott #1383.

The two individuals arrested were identified as John S. Pantages and Anthony D. Ferrara. When picked up they had a traveling case with them that contained the counterfeit stamps. Both subjects refused to provide any information to the authorities. It was never mentioned in the press but it is very likely that these men had been identified and subsequently arrested as a result of an Inspection Service investigation. It appears that under case number 12936-FI, Boston postal inspectors had been investigating these counterfeit jumbo stamps for some time. They had been identified as being sold in stamp-vending machines owned by the C&S Stamp Service.

On its surface this would seem to be a run-of-the-mill counterfeiting enterprise, except there were two notable points. The first was the stamp they picked to duplicate. This jumbo counterfeit was the first and possibly only known attempt to duplicate a commemorative rather than a regular issue stamp.[28] The other significant point was that these items were being sold out of vending machines. Now, all vending machine operators were not the minions of organized crime; still, this was a business very heavily influenced if not controlled by organized crime. Can you think of an easier way to launder money? Oh yes, there is another. It is called Las Vegas.

The Pot Boils

Between 1969 and 1971, stamp counterfeiting exploded on the East Coast. One common target identified was the 6-cent Eisenhower stamp. Many people would be arrested, and presses seized – yet these

28 John Hotchner in his U.S. Notes column in *Linn's* September 3, 2012 reported the possible counterfeit of Scott 894, the 3-cent Pony Express and Scott 896, the 3-cent Idaho Statehood.

were still large and successful criminal operations. On December 1, 1970, $530,000 in 6-cent Eisenhower stamps were seized when George Vios, Louis Angel, and Michael Granato were arrested at a Holiday Inn in Jersey City, New Jersey. Those arrests were the climax to what the Secret Service would describe as having been a month-long investigation. Seized with the stamps were two automobiles and a pistol.

These individuals had been plotting how they could maximize their profits by hitting the peak of the Christmas mailing season. The government knew this was the plan as one of their agents had posed as a buyer and negotiated the purchase of the stamps for that stated purpose.

When he went before the media, the United States attorney made a point of stating that to his knowledge there was no connection between this Jersey City case and the counterfeiting operation that just the month before had been closed down in North Bergen, New Jersey. That had been a currency case with the gang printing $50 and $100 bills, and it had been extensively covered in the media. The North Bergen case had been big. The agents found $250,000 worth of counterfeit currency, American Express money orders, traveler's checks, New Jersey drivers' licenses and the negatives for U.S. postage. It would have been nice if the U.S. Attorney had identified which stamp was involved here, but the suspicion was the 6-cent Eisenhower.

In reality, the United States Attorney's statement about cases not being connected was most likely misdirection. In February of 1971, under postal inspector case number 142167-MD, things really got going. In Flushing, New York, 3,000 counterfeit 6-cent Eisenhower stamps had been recovered with the arrest of Joseph Capasso and Frank DiGiorgia. Then on March 5, Salvatore Provenzano, the vice president of the International Brotherhood of Teamsters, was arrested. Provenzano, with five others, was charged with conspiracy to operate a counterfeiting operation that was printing currency, postage stamps, and food stamps. These arrests had not all gone down without incident. In one arrest there was a high-speed car chase through the streets of Jersey City. It only ended when one of the agents shot out the tires of the fleeing car.[29]

29 One thing that is continually pounded into your head in firearms training: do not shoot at fleeing vehicles. You do not know where your bullet is going to end up.

A four-count indictment was handed down charging six individuals with four counts. The charges were for possession of plates and photographic negatives to run off bogus $10 and $20 bills, 6-cent postage stamps, and $2 food coupons from the United States Department of Agriculture.[30] Tying the cases together, they were also charged with conspiracy to buy and then sell $250,000 in bogus $50 and $100 bills, which reportedly came from another counterfeiting operation.

Demonstrating both the significance of those involved, and the importance of the criminal enterprise, the announcement of these arrests was made in Washington by Attorney General John N. Mitchell. The indictment charged that Mr. Provenzano and Mr. Faugno supervised and financed this counterfeiting ring, while Mr. Andretta, Mr. Angelo and Mr. Gaugno oversaw the daily operations. Mr. Carlton and Mr. Friedman had been responsible for obtaining and then operating the equipment.

The indictment also accused Mr. Angelo with selling $249,300 in counterfeit $50 and $100 notes to a man identified by authorities as an undercover Secret Service agent. The money in this transaction was identified as coming from a printing plant in Port Chester that had been raided and seized in December. The arrests in Port Chester stemmed from a raid on November 24 of another printing company in North Bergen. It was reported that at that location, cameras and negatives for the production of counterfeits were uncovered. The report stated: "Some proofs were run off, but they were still in the embryo stage."

This investigation represents the work of the Secret Service Counterfeit Division at its best. Things apparently had gone down the way one would hope they would, and very seldom do. They had a lead and followed it step by step, putting the chain of events together. Using currency buys they moved through the maze of organized crime operations, tracing it to the highest levels.

Salvatore Provenzano was described as a close associate of Jimmy Hoffa, who was the president of the Teamsters Union. Salvatore was president of the state's 80,000 member Joint Teamsters Council, and

30 Postal inspectors reviewed the Food Stamp Redemption Center in the mid 1970s. It was found to be stuffed with counterfeit food stamps.

vice president of the national organization. He assumed that position when his brother, Anthony, went to prison for extorting $8,600 from a transportation company president. In July of 1975, Jimmy Hoffa would disappear; reportedly, he was on his way to meet Salvatore's brother Anthony in Detroit.

The Secret Service was wading in some very muddy waters here, but across the country various U.S. Attorneys were taking on organized crime. Nixon had given the Justice Department some new and powerful weapons. Possibly, this accounts for the very strange events that now occurred in this case. On July 2, the U.S. Attorney and a Federal Organized Crime Strike Force attorney called a press conference. They publicly stated that the Teamsters' chief had been cleared of all charges. The Federal Organized Crime Strike Force had been created under the Justice Department to identify and prosecute organized crime figures who up to this point no one seemed able to touch. That an attorney from the Strike Force was now suddenly going public and saying that Provenzano would not be prosecuted was not only unusual, it was unheard of. Obviously something a lot deeper was going on here. Suddenly, in Provenzano's stead, Salvatore Brigulio, the business agent for Teamsters Local 560, was arrested. Can you say *designated fall guy?* One wonders what kind of a deal Provenzano, an identified Mob kingpin, had struck.

This case was a really big deal, and simply because the Eastern end had been closed down, things were not over. In relationship to this, I would find an "Organized Vice Activity Report" dated August 1971. An informant had passed on information that "$60,000 in counterfeit 6-cent (Eisenhower) postage stamps and an unknown quantity of rare (stolen) stamps had been transported to Chicago" for distribution and sale. The Chicago connection was identified as Vincent Joseph Tedesso. This individual had an extensive record for burglary, fencing stolen goods, and bad checks. He was listed as a target for investigation by the Chicago Organized Crime Strike Force and in various postal investigations.

Any questions as to the accuracy of the informant information were removed when in May of 1973 counterfeit 6-cent Eisenhower stamps were identified in the Chicago area. Mail seizures were made and various amounts of counterfeit stamps were recovered.

Not surprisingly, however, the closer the investigation got to the local suppliers of the counterfeit stamps, the less cooperative the witnesses became.

It would be only later after some of the principle figures had died and some of the witnesses were given immunity to appear before the grand jury that the local (Chicago) cast of characters would be fully identified. The Strike Force report would state: "The following persons involved in this investigation were identified as being associates of organized crime: Vincent Tedesso, Leo Rugendorf, Angelo F. Taranto, Joseph E. Scoler, Irving Sidney Weiner and Harry S. Aleman." Harry Aleman would go on to notoriety as the syndicate's (Chicago's) man they sent to Las Vegas to oversee their investments. Eventually driven out of Las Vegas after freelancing in a jewel theft operation, he was ordered back to Chicago. He and his brother would be found in a shallow grave in an Indiana cornfield. Autopsies determined that when buried they had still been alive.

The case of the 6-cent Eisenhower personally brought home to me the fact that simply because a counterfeiter had been arrested or a press seized – that is not the end of the story. The revenue lost from a particular counterfeit stamp can linger for years. In April of 1977, I was screening rejected mail in the Chicago General Mail Facility. At the time I was looking for 13-cent Kennedy counterfeits. Imagine my surprise when I found before me counterfeit Eisenhower stamps still going through the mail. As late as 1990 these items were still being identified by knowledgeable and alert collectors.

Printing method used is photo offset lithography. The finely engraved detail is missing with the stamp demonstrating the flat surface noted in offset printing. Overall appearance of this stamp is good, but the coloration is darker than the original. It tends to be more bluish than gray. The perforation is 10.5 compared to the 11 X 10.5 on the government's product. Although produced on the East Coast, extensive use has been documented in the Midwest, especially in the Chicago area, zip code 606. It is believed that at least three different presses were used to produce this stamp.

1972: The 8-cent Eisenhower

The 8-cent Eisenhower stamp was issued on May 10, 1971, and within a year it was being counterfeited. On June 3, 1972, federal agents raided a printing plant in New York City that was running off both counterfeit currency and postage stamps. During this raid, five individuals were taken into custody along with the negatives that had been used to produce the counterfeit plates.

On June 26, 1972, a federal grand jury handed down indictments on a total of 10 men charging them with the counterfeiting of $950,000 in $10 bills and the 8-cent postage stamps. The government would identify the primary movers in this crime as Victor Sabatino and Arturo Ruemmely. It would be announced that although $500,000 in stamps had been printed, none of these items were ever distributed to the public.

Once again, either the public was being misled or the government officials were being delusional. Nearly two years later, in February of 1974, Donald Corman, an alert postal clerk at State College, Pennsylvania, spotted an envelope with what he thought was an 8-cent stamp that just did not look right. Looking again, he noted the envelope had gone through a canceling machine, but the cancel had ended up on the lower left corner of the cover. The machine did not target the stamp. This discrepancy had caused him to take a closer look. Suspecting a counterfeit, he brought it to the attention of his supervisor.

State College is the home of the American Philatelic Society, so the postmaster had a stamp authority he could readily turn to for advice. Contacted by the postmaster, the APS Executive Secretary James T. DeVoss was more than happy to take a look. After a brief inspection, Colonel DeVoss did not hesitate to declare that the stamp he was looking at was counterfeit.

One of the major reasons so many stamp collectors became members of the American Philatelic Society is the magazine that the organization issued. It was the authoritative voice for collectors in the United States. Not surprisingly it took no time at all for the existence of the counterfeit stamps to be trumpeted in their monthly publication. They also published a detailed description of the bogus item in their April issue.

> The genuine colors of Scott No. 1394 are bright and intense, whereas the black color of the counterfeit is dull and grayish. "EISENHOWER" on the genuine is a blue-gray. The counterfeit appeared to be a dull blue with a slight greenish cast. The "USA" on the genuine is red, whereas the counterfeit is red with a slight orange cast ...
>
> The word "EISENHOWER" and "USA" on the counterfeit stamp ... are not in alignment and they vary in distance from the portrait panel. It is obvious that they were printed in separate operations and not in one press run, as in the case of the genuine stamp ... The letters of "EISENHOWER" and "USA" on the genuine are sharp and well formed and the thickness of the strokes of the letters are poorly formed and the thickness of the strokes of the letters do not appear to be even and regular.
>
> The fine lines and small dots of the engraved portrait are clear and distinct on the genuine stamp, while the fine detail is missing from the lithographed counterfeit ...
>
> The paper used for the counterfeit is approximately the same color, but it appears to be thinner and slightly lighter than the genuine paper.
>
> The genuine stamp is perforated 11, whereas the counterfeit is perforated 12.5. The diameter of the perforation holes of the genuine is 1.0mm, while the perforation holes of the counterfeit are 0.8mm in diameter.

Not mentioned in the APS description were two other factors. The first hint was that the stamp was not cancelled. The post office had begun to mechanize mail-sorting operations in the 1950s, and one of the new tools at their disposal was the automatic facer canceller.

This was a technology that was triggered by the phosphor tagging then being put on postage stamps. The stamp on the questioned envelope had not been cancelled because the stamp had no phosphor tagging. The second glaring factor common to most all counterfeits is that the printing method used was lithographic or offset printing.

The cover had been mailed in Pittsburgh on February 12, 1974, and was addressed to Pennsylvania State University. The postal inspectors determined that this envelope had originated in Allentown, Pa. Case numbers assigned to this investigation were 62-16129-MD and 62-16130-MD. Small quantities of bogus stamps were recovered in each investigation, but obviously contrary to the government's assertions, not all of the counterfeit items had been seized before distribution occurred. No one really has any idea about how many of these stamps were distributed and eventually used in the mail.

The dam had finally given way. From the 1970s on, the U.S. Postal Service would find itself in a virtual battle for financial survival. The problem with postal reorganization is that suddenly they were expected to pay their own way. That meant they had to protect postal revenue. Mind you, the revenue lost to postal frauds would not be the cause of financial collapse, but it surely hasn't helped.

Genuine 8-cent Eisenhower, left, compared to its counterfeit

J. Edgar

Some parting thoughts on Mr. Hoover. He did take a second- or third-rate government department and meld it into one of the finest law enforcement organizations in the world. Still he was a man who it was not easy to work for. In the 1960s individual agents began to take on the Mob. Doing so, they put their jobs on the line. Hoover did not want them to do so. If you got on his bad side he did not forget.

Recently I was talking to an ex-agent who grew up in the FBI. His father was the Agent-in-Charge of a large West Coast city. One day he got a call from Hoover. He was upset about something a West Coast reporter had written and instructed the agent to contact the reporter and get him to retract his statement. After telling Hoover the best thing he could do is ignore the article, Hoover did not want to hear this. The agent was transferred to a small office in upper New York State.

4

Washington, We Have a Problem

As noted before, the 1960s had been a period of transition for the Postal Inspection Service. In the world of crime, the inspectors were facing challenges that rivaled the 1920s. As frequently happens, lessons that had been learned before were now forgotten. After the war years, there was a general aura of complacency, and by 1970 nearly all of the inspectors were rapidly approaching retirement. Work wise, the service was divided between those who did audits (the bean counters), and those who were given criminal assignments. At any given moment the dominant group changed with societal interests and criminal events. During the 1940s and 50s the bean counters had been in control. Then came the 1960s and a time of reckoning had arrived. The United States Post Office had again become every criminal's favorite target.

One straw that contributed to breaking the back of complacency was the Plymouth mail robbery. This was a crime that grabbed national attention. It was dubbed the largest robbery in the history of the United States. Somewhere in excess of $20 million in postal receipts were taken. The robbery was simplicity itself. A group of men stopped a mail truck on a lonely Cape Cod road that just happened to be transporting the weekly bank deposits from all the local Cape Post Offices to the Boston office.

The subsequent investigation was described as a comedy of errors. After many arrests there was a sensational trial that had the atmosphere of a circus. F. Lee Bailey, the noted defense attorney of the day, had a field day when he cross-examined the inspectors. Shortly thereafter it was time to appoint a new Chief Inspector. Violating tradition, William J. Cotter was brought in. Not only was this individual not from inside the Inspection Service, but he was coming over with a background in the OSS (Office of Strategic Services), CIA and worst of all, the FBI.

Cotter's appointment was not very popular with many of the old rank and file. This did not bother Cotter. He began a massive hiring program, recruiting from outside the Post Office from other federal agencies and intelligence services. Criminal investigation took precedence in training as well as a standardization of weapons. More importantly, inspectors were now expected to be proficient in their use. Coming from a background with job experience in the Post Office and then the intelligence community, I considered myself lucky to be recruited and hired. Only about one out of every 300 applicants was accepted.

After training in Washington, D. C., I was dispatched to a one-man office in North Texas. The philosophy was to throw the new guy into the fire and see how he would do. Directions from my new boss were simple. You will inspect x-number of Post Offices. Your domicile has been vacant for the last nine months. There are 75 cases on your desk waiting to be investigated – 20 of which are already overdue. I expect you to make two arrests each month. You have the inspector's manual (CIPI), a copy of postal regulations, and a phone. Now go and do your job.

Texas was an interesting three years of doing audits, keeping track of professional burglars, and working check and credit card fraud. To break any sense of monotony, there were controlled deliveries of narcotics, and at a moment's notice periodically being pulled out and sent on some surveillance assignment. Literally no two days were the same, and if you were a person addicted to a fixed schedule, this was not the job for you. This was also where I made my first counterfeit seizure – plates and currency being shipped from California to Texas.

As a new inspector, your first three years are considered a probationary training period. Reaching that milestone, it was time to move on. With the option of following either an audit or criminal track, I requested a criminal assignment. I had no desire to spend the rest of my life counting stamps or computing 2nd class postage. Shortly after the request went in, the phone rang and I was told to pack my bags and report to Chicago. At the time I would have no idea this would lead me into the world of counterfeit stamps and even currency counterfeiters.

In Chicago my assignment was everything I could desire. Officially I was assigned to "external" crimes on the South Side of

Chicago. This covers all the crimes committed on the Post Office and its employees by people who were not themselves employees. In the years I was there, this would involve check and credit card theft (stolen from the mail), assaults, robberies, burglaries, and even an occasional sexual assault. Oh and yes, there was even an occasional homicide or two thrown in. It involved developing a strong rapport with the cop on the beat as well as developing other not-so-savory sources of information, or as one of my coworkers once said, "You do not find swans in a sewer."

If I wanted to get into the world of stamp counterfeiting, requesting an assignment to Chicago was a good idea. I would discover that Chicago, and New York, are the epicenters for this activity. I would soon conclude that for some time the U.S. Postal Service had been systematically under attack. What I found truly amazing was that it appeared few of the folks in charge seemed to realize this fact.

Compounding the Post Office's problems, this organization was in a battle for survival on a number of fronts. There were political attacks, fighting with militant labor unions, and losing market share to private delivery services. Aggravating attempts to protect postal revenue, on the public's part there was increasing resentment at escalating postage rates. Both individuals and businesses began to seriously look for ways to cut their postage expenses. Increasingly they would turn to contraband postage – counterfeit, washed stamps, bogus postage meters. Postal management slowly had to be dragged into recognizing that combating revenue fraud was a problem that needed attention.

Shelbyville, Indiana

May 1974, 4,000 counterfeit 6-cent Eisenhower stamps simulating Scott #1393 were recovered from "stamp dealers" at Shelbyville. This incident is most likely related to the $60,000 in counterfeit 6-cent stamps reportedly transported in the early 1970s from the East Coast to Chicago, as mentioned previously (August 1971, Organized Crime Activity Report). Northwest Indiana was very much under the thumb of the "Outfit" in Chicago.

Philadelphia, Pennsylvania

July 1974, Case #62-18766-MD – 100,000 counterfeit Jefferson Memorial stamps (Scott #1510) were recovered. Charles C. Meeks was arrested. No other information is publicly known. Most likely the arrest of Charles Meeks led to the following case.

Philadelphia, Pennsylvania

September 1974, Case #62-18840-MD – 361,759 counterfeit stamps (Jefferson Memorial) were recovered. The list of arrestees was William D. Dixon, Joseph DeFino, John J. McCoy, William J. McCoy, and William E. Owens. Leslie John Bell was arrested for passing $5 food stamps, which also had been counterfeited by this group.

Maryville, Tennessee

June 1975, Case 6236958-MD – 337,715 counterfeit stamps were recovered, along with printing equipment used by the gang. Arrested were James Charlton, his son Mark, Frank Royce, Donald Lee Mowie, and James F. Swartz. Two of the witnesses in this case were killed in what the authorities would identify as a murder/suicide. The 50-cent Lucy Stone Stamp (Scott #1293) was the primary target of this group's endeavor. It was reported that this operation had also printed and distributed 30-cent and $1 stamps.

I was assigned to Chicago, so I didn't know very much about counterfeiting operations in Tennessee, or for that matter other locations. The Inspection Service was never really very good at talking across either divisional or regional boundaries. The first time I took notice of what had occurred in Maryville was when a blurb appeared in the Inspection Service Bulletin.

> On June 25, 1975, Postal Inspectors and Secret Service agents executed a search warrant at the offices of the DBD Corporation at Maryville, Tn. Approximately $170,000 in counterfeit fifty-cent U.S. postage stamps, a printing press, counterfeit plates and a quantity of other

paraphernalia used in the counterfeiting operation were seized. Two offenders were arrested on the same day and three co-conspirators were apprehended later. One of the persons arrested stated that counterfeit stamps were to be used to mail cocaine after it was flown in from Mexico and South America. The mailings were to be from a point in Arizona to New York, Chicago, Denver, and Miami. The reason so large a denomination stamps was counterfeited was that it was intended to put sufficient postage on each shipment of drugs to make the mailing first class and therefore not subject to examination without a search warrant. On December 19 and 20, 1975 a trial was held for all five defendants. One man pled guilty and was sentenced to one year in prison followed by five years probation, the remaining four offenders were found guilty of manufacturing and possession of counterfeit postage stamps. Three received five year prison terms and one was sentenced to five years probation.

When a reporter from the Washington Post heard this story, he decided to follow through on the narcotics angle and flesh out the story. In a story written by Mike Causey on November 12, 1976, he revealed more about the drugs featured in this case. According to his report, the intention had been to transport those drugs from Mexico into secure bases they had already established in Arizona. The gang had concluded that getting the drug shipments into this country would not be all that difficult. They were just taking a page from what was already occurring in Florida; their plan was to use low-flying radar evading aircraft. One has only to remember that at this time the nation's borders could best be described as a sieve.

The truly new angle introduced by the group was the planned use of counterfeit stamps to facilitate transportation inside the United States. They had concluded that a great way to handle their distribution was via the U.S. mail.[31] Their reasoning was really very sound. After all, the mail would be reasonably fast and safe. Additionally, if they sent their shipments via first class, their parcels could not be intercepted or opened for inspection without a search warrant. Their downfall was the decision to make their own stamps.

31 Over the years many drug smugglers would reach this same conclusion. At one point the inspectors ran a survey of parcels leaving Hawaii for the states. They determined that about 80 percent of the parcels they inspected contained some quantity and variety of narcotics.

Not being printers themselves, they reached out to someone they knew. This man had learned the printing craft while incarcerated in the Atlanta Federal Penitentiary for bank robbery. At the time he was a resident of Maryville, Tennessee.

Another part of the story that appeared in the press concerned the sharp-eyed postal clerk who reportedly spotted the bogus stamps on a package. It had been reported that when notified the inspectors moved in. As usual, the story being told may have been more than a little fiction than fact. In the real story another individual who was peripherally connected to the gang found himself under arrest for, of all things, cattle rustling. Believe it or not, this is an offense still taken seriously in many parts of the country, and he decided he wanted to strike a deal. He called the Secret Service and said, "Ah, folks, something is going on you might want to know about." To prove his point, he arranged for a postal inspector and a Secret Service agent to see two suitcases full of stamps in an Atlanta hotel room. The stamp the agents saw was the 50-cent Lucy Stone.[32]

Now this informant had the agent's full attention. They would follow the two suitcases to South Florida where sometime later three members of the gang would be arrested. The investigation in Florida established the seized stamps had been destined for use in South Florida for the distribution of incoming narcotics shipments. The informant identified Maryville, Tennessee as the location where the stamps were being printed. In Maryville, a team of Secret Service agents and postal inspectors began a surveillance of what they identified as the location of the printing plant. This surveillance was very low key because their target, the DBM Corporation, was located directly across the street from the local newspaper. The local police, the sheriff, and even the federal Marshall Service had not been informed of this surveillance, or that any investigation was ongoing. Maryville was a tight little community and the thinking was that if one of the locals found out anything, it would take about five minutes for everyone in town to know it.

Still, the agents were having difficulty establishing probable cause for a search warrant, but fortunately their informant would

32 It is ironic that the Lucy Stone stamp was picked. She was a pioneer suffragette and a leader of the temperance movement.

once again come to their aid. He and his girlfriend (also a pillar of society) supplied the agents with an affidavit that they had heard the pounding of a printing press coming from the location under surveillance. In reality, one or more of the agents had the very strong suspicion that their informant had broken into the building in question to verify the printing press was actually there. Needless to say, this bit of information would never appear in the affidavit the agents presented for their search warrant.

The magistrate signed the warrant, and that night when the agents entered the building, they found the printing press with all its associated equipment and supplies. Then, in a back room, they found something else. Gathered in a number of large trash bags was all the printing waste left over from the last printing run. When James Charlton, the primary printer, entered the building, he was arrested. Then his son, Mark, was picked up at their home.

Postal Inspector Robert Tittle was the primary case agent, and with his counterpart in the Secret Service, they processed and interviewed the prisoners. Tittle, at one time or another, would be present for the processing and interview of each of the defendants in this case. At the trial, he would be able to give continuity to the testimony that tied all of the pieces of the investigation together.

From a legal standpoint, in the interview with James Charlton, an interesting incident occurred. When he was given his Miranda rights, he immediately said he wanted an attorney. After all, this was not his first time in the batter's box. According to the rules, right here as an agent you are supposed to stop your interrogation. *It does not always happen that way.*[33]

"Just visiting," Tittle went on to explain to James how they had his son cold. If they were really lucky maybe they could share the same cell in Atlanta. Needless to say, this got James's attention. Before long he was going into great detail about how he had done everything, and

33 Probably should not tell this story, but I had a similar experience. I was investigating a shooting and the victim's girlfriend was found with about 50 Treasury checks. It was a deal that had gone wrong. She called her attorney who after talking to his client said, "I don't want you to talk." After he left we were "visiting," just telling her what was going to happen next. I told her we would treat the checks for fingerprints. Rhetorically I asked, will we find your prints on these checks? Do I need to say what happened next? The appeals court sustained the conviction and the admission of her verbal confession. Yes, her fingerprints were on the checks, as well as her mother's, who just happened to be a postal clerk.

how his son was totally innocent of any involvement. Unfortunately for both James and his son this story did not match the facts. All the seized items would be sent to the Inspection Service crime laboratory for processing. When examined, the Atlanta lab found the fingerprint impressions of Mark Charlton in the inked stamp impression. This was not just once, but a number of times.

Court exhibit at trial of fingerprint ink impression on top of stamp

It turned out that Agent Tittle had plenty of time to talk to James and Mark Charlton. The local U.S. marshal was in the process of running for county sheriff and he had been less than happy with what had gone down. When called, he refused to take custody of the prisoners. Inspector Tittle would later relate that things were strained even with the local newspaper. It was located directly across the street from where all the action had taken place, yet not a word about either the raid or investigation would appear in the local newspaper.

I have developed a great affection for defendants who insist on going to trial. This creates a paper trail. When this trial started out, there were five defendants, one of whom was Donald J. Howie. He soon changed his plea to guilty and would fully cooperate with the government. The agents really thought that Howie's involvement with the crime was minimal, and in return for his testimony, they would try to intercede on his behalf with the judge. Most times this works but in this case it did not. The judge in this trial was a hard-nosed law and order type. His idea of leniency was to give Howie one year in prison followed by five years of probation. Howie would die in prison.

The other four defendants pushed things all the way to the end. Inspector Tittle, the person who had interviewed all of the defendants, would play a starring role in the trial. The judge, with a no- nonsense control of his courtroom, would forcefully remind Tittle of the rules governing the use of codefendant testimony. Having all four defendants, each with their own attorney, also provided moments of levity to the trial. At one point one attorney was conducting a cross-examination of the fingerprint identification. This was the fingerprint found on the stamps sheets. At the conclusion of the testimony one defense attorney turned to the other and sarcastically commented, "Well, that helped a lot." The cross-examination had the effect of imprinting on the jury's mind that his client had taken an active part in the production of the counterfeit stamps.

In the end, the evidence was more than overwhelming. After a two-day trial, all the defendants were found guilty. James Charlton had tried valiantly to protect his son, but in the end Mark would be sentenced to five years of probation on two counts of counterfeiting. The other three defendants were sentenced to five years on each of two counts, which were to run concurrently. The ultimate price may have been paid by the two government informants; Wise and his girlfriend, Cross, were both found dead in a South Florida motel room. On the police blotter, those deaths were listed as a murder/suicide that some believe may or may not actually have been the case. Remember, this was in the middle of the Miami drug wars and bodies littered the streets. These folks had just helped screw up a major drug operation. Neither the Mafia nor the Colombians were exactly known for their forgiving nature.

When the government finally tallied up the amount of stamps seized, it was acknowledged that $167,857 in the counterfeit 50-cent stamps had been taken off the streets. Probably of much more importance was the disruption it may have provided to narcotics distribution from both Florida and the Southwest. There was another significant point that slipped by me for some time. Besides the Lucy Stone stamps, it had been reported that this group was also printing the then current 30-cent and $1 stamp. The agents reportedly seized the press, perforator, plates, plate-making equipment, and enough waste paper to fill a large mail truck. Any way you look at this case the investigation was a success.

Still, even after their conviction the defendants did not give up. They took not just one, but three bites on the judicial apple. James Charlton filed an appeal again, and again, and again.

• • •

In the UNITED STATES OF AMERICA V. JAMES ARTHUR CHARLTON et al. the validity of the search warrant was challenged. The trial judge had dismissed the motion to suppress the evidence seized in the search of the DBD Corporation located at 214 East Harper Street, Maryville, Tennessee. Charlton challenged the reliability of the government's informant information used to support the warrant and the use of double hearsay in the affidavit the agent filed to obtain the warrant. This was also where the information was brought forward about the little matter of a suspicious broken rear window where someone (the informant?) just may have entered the building to determine if evidence of the printing plant was still there.

Because both the informants had died in a Florida motel, to defend its actions, the government was no longer in a position to produce their informants to answer these charges. To respond, the only thing the government could do was to use the direct testimony of one of the agents. Special Agent Ronald E. Seimanski presented the following factual grounds:

> Mr. Jim Wise, Huntsville, Alabama, provided information to Postal Inspector L. G. Weaver and Paul Cummerford ...on June 18, 1975 that he saw in the possession of Donald Lee Howie and Jimmy Swartz, two (2) suitcases and that the suitcases were opened in his presence and he saw the two suitcases contained sheets of U.S. Postage Stamps ... The postage stamps had no border or plate number and were in loose sheets and not

bound in any manner ... Swartz further related the counterfeit 50-cent stamps had been and were being produced by Jim Charlton at or near Maryville, Tennessee.

To substantiate the information supplied by their informant, the Secret Service verified that on May 2, 1975, Charlton had purchased 8,000 sheets of white gummed paper cut to 9"x10.5." They also verified that James Charlton had been attempting to locate, and then had purchased a perforator that would make round holes as opposed to long slits. Additionally, Mac Vean K. Sweazey, an agent, testified that when he was standing outside the building at 214 East Harper Street, he had heard a printing press in operation. Tying James Charlton and his son to the printing plant, surveillance agents would testify that on many occasions they observed Mr. James Charlton and his son, Mark, entering and leaving the premises they were watching.

For the warrant, the government argued the "double hearsay rule" did not apply. Independent confirmation had been obtained to support what the informant was telling them, and such testimony could be considered in a probable cause determination. The affiant recited that Wise "had developed additional information" (burglarizing the building?) that linked the alleged counterfeiting operation to 214 East Harper Street, the address of DBD Corporation. The nature of this "additional information" was never identified to the court. For corroboration they used the statement provided by Agent Swartz that the stamps were being produced at or near Maryville, Tennessee.

The court rules that "the affidavit, taken as a whole, provides sufficient underlying circumstances from which the magistrate could conclude that a criminal offense was probably being, or had been committed on the premises to be searched, and that the particular items to be seized would probably be found on the premises." It is very seldom that a federal judge or magistrate will throw out a properly prepared and executed federal search warrant.[34]

Still, the defendants were not done. On November 30, 1976, the

34 Frequently this consideration even extends into local courts. Many times we would shop cases in local Chicago courts. Time and again local cases would be thrown out. When our cases were called they would fly through the system. It may have helped that some of the warrants were prepared by a new assistant U.S. Attorney named Scott Turow.

conviction was again appealed, and a decision was handed down on October 21, 1977. The three defendants had appealed their conviction for the forging and counterfeiting the 50-cent stamps. The foundation of this appeal rested on their contention that when James Arthur Charlton was in custody, the oral confession extracted by the agents had not been voluntary, and should have been excluded.

The argument was that on June 25, 1975, Charlton was arrested without a warrant. Earlier that evening, special agents of the United States Secret Service (and postal inspectors) pursuant to a search warrant, entered offices rented by Charlton at 214 East Harper Street in Maryville, Tn. At that location they seized a large quantity of counterfeit stamps and the paraphernalia used in manufacturing those items. Upon his arrest Charlton was taken to the courthouse in Knoxville, Tennessee, where he was fingerprinted and otherwise processed. They argued that it was two hours after the arrest that Charlton was finally advised of his constitutional rights. Charlton declined to sign a written waiver of those rights and instead told the agents he wanted an attorney. He expressed no desire to talk to the agents.

It was shortly after 1 a.m. when Special Agent Mac Vean K. Sweazey came into the room and said, "Well, got your son up here. What are you going to do about that?" That is when Charlton began to make the incriminating statements that would later be used against him. This interrogation continued until about 3 a.m., and in the course of this interrogation, no attorney was ever procured for Charlton and he never signed any written statement related to the counterfeiting operation.

At a pre-trial suppression hearing, Charlton stated the following:

> A: I talked to the postal inspector (Tittle) and Mr. Sweazey. I told them I would talk to them but only thing, clear everybody out of the room and what I was going to say would be off the record.
>
> Q: Listen to my question. Did you speak to them of your own free will?
>
> A: Not really. They actually got me mad because they kept hinting to the fact I didn't care anything about my son, and they actually used my son until they got me mad, really.

At the conclusion of the hearing, the trial judge ruled that

Charlton's statement could still go to the jury. He ruled that what Charlton had said was not the result of coercion. The statements he had made were simply the result of his anger with the agents.

The appeals court seriously considered and weighed Charlton's arguments. Again, they would conclude that in their judgment his desire to protect his son did not render his confession involuntary, nor did it necessitate a finding that it had been coerced. They further concluded that the admissibility of statements obtained after the person in custody has decided to remain silent, under the Miranda decision, depends on whether his "right to cut off questioning" was "scrupulously honored." The final judgment was that in this instance, the continued questioning of Charlton fell within the scope of being a "harmless error." With or without Charlton's statement, the court ruled that this would not have affected the outcome of the trial. In the court's view, the evidence was overwhelming.

The court stated their conclusions as such: Secret Service Agent Seimanski testified that several thousand sheets of the counterfeit stamps were seized as well as the press, a hole perforator, plates, and other paraphernalia used in the stamp production. Charlton's fingerprints were found on some of those sheets of stamps and plates, and there was no doubt that he fully controlled the premises on East Harper Street. Although Charlton's son had technically rented the building housing the DBD Corporation, the second installment of the rent was paid by the senior Charlton. Numerous suppliers of materials and equipment testified that Charlton had also made those purchases. Considering all of the above, the testimony that related to the incriminating statement, while received at the trial was not unduly emphasized by the prosecution: "The court being of the opinion that in all other respects the defendants received a fair trial, free from any prejudicial error, the judgment of the district court is affirmed."

Looking back at the Maryville case, some final thoughts come to mind. I am torn about how to treat both Charlton Sr. and Jr. Taking a page from how Agent Motto treated the defendants in his book, the temptation was to change names to protect the guilty if not the innocent. Sometimes people make bad decisions and get caught up in things that maybe they should not have. At the same time if you have been arrested, convicted, and then had some degree of punishment, you have paid your price, and by bringing these issues up again, one can be inflicting more pain and suffering on individuals who may have paid the price and possibly turned their life around. In this case I was painted into the corner by the court record.

James Charlton would probably be categorized as a career criminal. He apparently spent time in the penitentiary for bank robbery. That was before he entered the world of counterfeiting, so he was hardly an innocent bystander in this case. Yet, one must give him credit for his attempts to shield his son from any judicial action. It can be argued that his son most likely would not have been involved unless invited in, and his father was, after all, teaching him a trade. We do tend to follow in our father's footsteps, and sometimes we learn from their mistakes.

Another factor in Charlton's defense, he was far from being the mastermind behind this project. He was contract labor, and if things had gone as planned would have received 50 percent of the profits from these stamps. That, or a bullet in the back of his head. It is known that he was petrified of someone. When Inspector Tittle testified, he tried to get this into his testimony as mitigating information, but the judge would have none of it.

These stamps had been made to facilitate the transportation of narcotics across the United States. The people involved had a propensity towards violence. In Florida, bodies were dropping like raindrops and coincidentally three of the primary players in this case would soon be dead. Maybe it was murder, suicide, heart attack, but then again, just a thought.

Another little gem was found in the transcript of the trial: "Mr. Royce, if I did not hear Mr. Durand correctly, why I stand to be corrected, but did Mr. Durand, in going over your past (criminal) record, indicate that on January 7, 1959, you had a matter involving counterfeiting Post Office stamps in Allegheny County, Pennsylvania, which is Pittsburgh?" WHAT??? (Remember those stamps found alongside the road in 1960? It was also introduced in the trial that down in Florida the government had used electronic surveillance on Mr. Royce. Besides printing stamps it appears that Charlton had been contracted to also print what agents would describe as an adult book (pornography). This also was a market very much controlled by organized crime. When the delivery of this material was delayed, monitored phone conversations showed that a "contract" had been put out on both Francis Swartz and his wife.

Are you wondering who the truly bad guy was in this whole drama? My bet would be on Frank J. Jacek, aka Frank Royce. He was the Florida connection and appears to be the glue that was holding everything together. His involvement with the previous Pittsburgh counterfeiting operation speaks volumes just by itself. His response in court to this accusation was, "Who me? I was just an innocent bystander."

Chicago – the 10-cent Crossed Flag

The Education of an Inspector and

A Case that Began to Change Attitudes

By 1975, I was in Chicago assigned to external crimes. This assignment would cover a multitude of sins. External crimes primarily means crimes committed on the Post Office and its employees by people who are not employees. Assigned to the South Side of Chicago, most of my time was spent working check and credit card theft and forgery cases with an occasional robbery thrown in. All the inspectors in Chicago external crimes were fairly new to the game so we did not think twice about trying new things. We worked the street for informants, and began to make undercover buys. We did this on our own without a whole lot of oversight or permission from Washington. We were producing arrests and the thought was it is always easier to say "sorry" than to get official permission on operations that some might think were controversial.

To interrupt this happy state of affairs, one day a counterfeit case popped up. I was drafted as one of the worker bees assigned to do basic interviews and to chase down leads. More importantly, I had the pleasure of watching and learning from senior inspectors who really knew how to put together a complex criminal investigation. If one had to take a tutorial, this was the way to do it.

This Chicago case was not the work of some established gang, or even a professional criminal. Rather, it originated in the mind of, and was carried out in the home basement of just an ordinary guy who simply saw an opportunity to make some extra cash for Christmas. The ease with which his crime was carried out, and the ready market found on the streets of Chicago would grab the attention of both postal management and the Inspection Service. The impact of the thinking in Washington possibly helped to prepare the foundation for what would eventually become known as the Contraband Postage Identification Program.

What happened in Chicago can best be described as a handyman's approach to stamp manufacturing. Apparently one day while looking at a sheet of the 10-cent postage stamp, Heinz Burg thought, "Hey, I could make these." Besides, Christmas was coming up and he concluded that everyone could use a little extra cash for the holidays. His thinking was that he could make money printing these items, and his customers would also be able to save some money on their Christmas mailing. Everybody wins – except the Post Office.

With all the single color stamps the Bureau of Engraving had pushed out in the last 100 years, it is a mystery why Burg decided to duplicate the 10-cent crossed flag stamp. Most likely this was simply because this was the then current stamp of the day for first-class postage. For production purposes it did complicate things. This stamp had two colors. With a simple offset press this meant that for each color you had to make a separate printing plate, and each sheet had to go through the press twice. Then, when you are doing the actual printing this can lead to alignment problems.[35]

On a sizable number of stamp sheets, Burg would have alignment problems. Then when he ran his printed sheets through the 36-inch Nygren-Dahly vertical perforator he had purchased, he would have alignment problems here as well. The end result was that, yes, he printed stamps he could sell, but also a large amount of printing waste. Not wishing to just put this out in his own trash, Burg's solution was to dump the garbage bags full of scrap in a nearby Chicago public park. When a bag of trash was found by a curious citizen, it would be the tip off to the post office that it had a problem

35 Even the professionals at the Bureau of Engraving have had this problem. This is demonstrated by the numerous errors which over the years found their way onto the market and into collector hands. For the government, eventually this would be solved with the evolution of printing technology. For the counterfeiter, it is the computer and quality color copiers that solved this problem.

on its hands. This discovery would trigger an investigation involving just about the entire Chicago division of the postal inspectors.

To say that postal managers were flustered when a little old lady walked into the Post Office with a shopping bag full of scrap counterfeit stamps is an understatement. This was going into the Christmas mailing season and even at the best of times this could be a significant problem. The immediate response was to scream for help. After all, for the last 100 years, the Secret Service had forcefully claimed this as their jurisdiction. Possibly, the Inspector in Charge's first thought was let them burn up their man-hours. The problem was, the Secret Service is not all that interested in stamps. The response came back – ah, sorry we have this thing going on called an election, and we are busy with our protection duties. *You can just gather everything up and we will send someone over in the spring to pick things up. We will take a look then.* You can imagine how that went over.

At that time there were about 140 inspectors in the Chicago office, and in one capacity or another just about every one of them would be drafted to investigate this case. The lead inspectors were Fraud Team leaders Jim McCarthy and Karl Kell. Over the years they had demonstrated the ability to tackle the most complex criminal cases. Until this stamp case was over it would be the primary investigative priority for the division.

In tackling the case, a systematic approach was taken. One group of agents, primarily auditors, were assigned to review the incoming collection mail to see if any counterfeit stamps could be identified going through the system. Any question about how these stamps were being used was promptly answered. Inspectors checking the mail found hundreds and even thousands of mailing envelopes bearing the counterfeit stamps. With mailers identified, these names were turned over to external crime inspectors (such as myself) and our assignment was running down and interviewing the mailers. Our questions were simple: Where did you get the stamps? How much did you pay? Do you have any of these items left? On more than one occasion we had to argue additional unused stamps out of the hands of mailers who suddenly recognized these items could have collector's value.

Another group of inspectors, primarily the fraud investigators, were given the job of running down printing equipment and perforators. Special attention was given to anyone who may have been recently shopping for a round-hole perforator. The sale of offset presses may have been common, but perforators are another story. This is an obsolete technology and perforator sales are few and far apart. Not only printing supply houses but just about every printing business in Chicago was visited. Ink suppliers were identified and then samples of the paper used for the stamps were taken to the Institute of Paper Chemistry in Appleton, Wisconsin. They identified the type of gummed paper being used. Then the tedious job of checking for the sale of this paper began.

In the mailer interviews, there would be some unusual twists and turns. Many individuals would insist they had purchased their stamps at the local Post Office. The immediate suspicion was that these folks were just blowing smoke, but just to be sure, inspectors were assigned to physically check not only the postal main stock, but also the stamp stock in every sales window in Chicago. No counterfeit stamps were found in the Post Office stamp stock, but they were traced back to the Post Office. It was found that a uniformed postal carrier was selling the counterfeit stamps out of the back of his mail truck.

The investigation determined the distribution of the counterfeits began about November 27th. Eventually it would be established that many of those who claimed, "I bought them at the Post Office," had a different source. In more than a few cases this was coming from the printer's relatives who he was also using as his primary distributors. The sale of the stamps concluded about one week prior to Christmas when the news of the investigation leaked out, and a newspaper story appeared telling how the inspectors were once again investigating a stamp counterfeiting case in the Chicago area. Considering the hundreds of individuals being interviewed it was inevitable that someone would talk to a reporter.

In the investigation, the trail of stamp sales had not been all that hard to follow. Soon all the pieces of the puzzle began to point in one direction. Purchases of gummed paper, printing equipment, and the sales of stamps would eventually all point to Heinz Burg as the person who was the source of the bogus items. Burg's idea of a distribution network had been to give the stamps to his relatives who in turn would sell them literally door-to-door. Some of these folks even supplied stamps to their employers, which I am sure improved their employment standings. I amusingly referred to Burg's distribution plan as the Girl Scout cookie method of distribution.

The story of how the printing equipment was tracked down injected another note of levity into the investigation. While the stamp sales were being traced back to their sources, the inspectors got a call from one of the printing equipment supply houses they had previously visited. At the time, this individual had claimed that he had no knowledge of any suspicious sales. His memory suddenly improved when the check Burg had given him to rent a printing press and round hole perforator bounced. Then, when this individual went and repossessed his equipment, he found what one might call incriminating evidence. On the ink roller for the press was a printing blanket with the impression of a crossed flag stamp sheet. Not being the tidiest of individuals, there also were all kinds of printing scraps jammed into every nook and cranny of the machine.

Probably feeling close to being the subject of an indictment for obstruction and giving false statements to a federal agent, and now stuck with a bad check, the owner of this printing supply company suddenly decided that he wanted to be the government's star witness. The authorities would welcome his information, but it can be fair to say they were less than pleased with his previously demonstrated degree of cooperation. Supplying counterfeiting equipment was hardly a new experience for this individual. Checking Secret Service records, it was found this was the third counterfeiting operation where the equipment used by the perpetrators had come out of his inventory. He was indeed walking on very thin legal ice and getting a pass, in this case, came with a price. For all intents and purposes, in the future he would take on a new silent business partner - - the government.

Armed with the evidence turned over from the printing equipment dealer, and the mailer interviews, more than enough information had been collected to support a search warrant for Burg's house. He was picked up and his house searched. In his basement the inspectors found two perforating machines, the printing plates used to print the stamps, and over 470,000 completed stamps. In excess of 950,000 stamps would finally be recovered from Burg and from his identified distributors.

If this case demonstrated anything, it was that the revenue of the Post Office was vulnerable to just about anyone. Entering a guilty plea, Burg would be sentenced to 120 days in a work-release program. This would be followed with probation for a period of two years and eight months. This investigation had been a success, but events would show it had done nothing to discourage this activity. News of this case had been splashed all over both local and national media, and it is safe to assume that a number of others would suddenly think – *Why not?*

Another unfortunate outcome of this investigation was that it placed a strain on the relationship that existed between the Secret Service and the Inspection Service. Historically the inspectors had almost always taken a back seat to the Secret Service when a counterfeiting case was being investigated, and we were the supporting cast. As these cases are incredibly labor intensive it was easy for postal management to step aside and let the other agency carry the ball. Besides that, the abilities and resources the Secret Service could bring to a case could not be questioned. Now, however, things had changed. It would become obvious, even to Washington, that we were being bombarded with one case after another. The management of the Inspection Service would be forced to recognize that these investigations were significant and needed postal attention.

If a revenue case is not crushed fast it can have a negative impact on both the public's perceptions, and the financial integrity of the Postal Service. After Postal Reorganization in 1970, financial integrity would become a significant issue for the postal establishment. Now, as an independent government agency, the postal service was expected to live on the revenue it generated. No longer could the U.S. Treasury be counted on as a piggy bank for the Post Office. It is amazing how this could focus attention – even with postal bureaucrats.

Dayton, Ohio – 13-cent Liberty Bell

Breaking New Ground

Anyone who has ever watched a police drama is aware of the importance informants play in police work. In reality, unless you are nabbed at the scene of the crime, informants provide the leads that solve many crimes. CSI and your crime lab may give you the evidence to prove a case in court, but the lead to make that arrest frequently comes from your informants.

In the spring of 1976, in Dayton, Ohio, an informant who was working for a local police detective walked in and showed the detective several strips of what appeared to be the then-current 13-cent Liberty Bell stamp. There were only four stamps on each strip. The informant told the detective the stamps were counterfeit, and they were being produced locally.

Apparently in Dayton, a group of individuals decided to make their own copy of the 13-cent Liberty Bell. Being a single-color stamp it was an easy item to duplicate. This would be one of three known times this particular stamp would be the target of counterfeit activity. The other two instances were in Boston and New York respectively. What would make the Dayton effort stand out was the apparent attempt to make their copy at least look like a legitimate coil stamp.

The Liberty Bell stamp produced by the government was only manufactured in either a booklet or coil format. The significance of this was that on every legitimate Liberty Bell stamp there should be either one or two straight edges. The average counterfeiter concerned with easy production is not going to worry about a little detail like this. It is a lot less labor intensive to just run off your stamps in a sheet format.

In the other two attempts at duplicating the 13-cent Liberty Bell, the easy field test was simply to look at the stamp edges. If your stamp is perforated on all four sides, it is a counterfeit. That did not stop thousands or even possibly millions of these items from going through the mail. Then along comes Dayton, Ohio. This stamp was in a strip format with both the top and bottom edges being a straight edge – not perforated. Why they went to this effort, I have absolutely no idea.

When the local detective had this case dumped into his lap, he had already been working on an investigation that involved the printing of counterfeit business checks. In his case he had already identified Mr. James Woodhouse Jr. and the Orr Printing Company as being the probable source of these items. Tens of thousands of dollars in very realistic business checks were being used to victimize both local merchants and financial institutions. Now his informant was telling him that the very folks he was looking at had branched out.

The detective promptly screamed for help. Both the postal inspectors and the Secret Service were notified and came to the detective's assistance. What followed was an excellent example of all these organizations working together. Focusing on the Orr Printing Company, the first thing they had to do was develop probable cause supporting a federal search warrant.

The primary directive in the care and feeding of informants is to protect their existence. You do this by hiding their identity. If you get them killed, you cannot use them again, not to mention the impact this would have on your efforts to recruit other informants. It is preferable to do this by developing independent information that supports what they tell you so their identity is not exposed in your affidavit for your warrant. To provide this protection, besides their surveillance, the agents targeted the paper and the perforator.

The paper was identified as Tro-Mark II Grade 801, Lot #5, and the only local supplier was the Walker Paper Company. Checking sales, the agent found the only recent sale of this product was to the Orr Printing Company. Agents then established that a perforator capable of making the exact same holes found on the bogus stamps had also recently been purchased by the Orr Printing Company. Probable cause had been established, and now all the agents needed to establish was that stamps were being sold or used.

This occurred on July 26, when four envelopes originating from one mailer were found in the mail. Then on July 30, another envelope from a different mailer was discovered. This may not have been much, but it was all the agents needed. On August 2nd, three search warrants were simultaneously executed. The targets were the Orr Printing Company and the residences of the two identified mailers.

At the print shop, the agents hit pay dirt. They found a rubber printing blanket that still had the impressions of the 13-cent Liberty Bell stamp on it. Then they matched the gummed paper in the shop to that used for the stamps. Even a photo negative with the impression of the bell holder was identified. The Orr Printing Company was officially established as the site of a counterfeiting operation. What this meant was that just about everything inside the walls could and would be impounded by the agents as evidence.

Searching the residences produced few results. At one location, there were just a few hundred stamps. At the other, no stamps were found, and the story given by the occupant was that while he had been at a local bar he needed a stamp for a letter. He claimed that an unknown benefactor had supplied it for him. Although the agents could not prove otherwise, they felt the veracity of this statement was seriously in question. This skepticism was only reinforced when in the search conducted on this house agents found 20 bogus driver's licenses in various names.

The primary players in this little drama had been identified as Charles Wiley Orr, James Woodhouse Jr., and James Lee Kayser. When the Assistant U.S. Attorney was informed of the results of the searches he immediately authorized the arrests of all three individuals.

The government's attorney commented that Orr was arrested because he owned the print shop. Woodhouse's arrest was based on being identified as the seller of the counterfeit stamps. Kayser's misfortune was that he had been observed both working the printing equipment, and also years before he had a record of his being part of a similar counterfeiting operation.[36] The latter is a point the Post Office has never grasped. When one is a skilled counterfeiter, to continue in one's chosen lifestyle, you normally do not pick up another criminal endeavor – say, like bank robbery.

This case was given some coverage by the Ohio newspapers. Postal Inspector Jerry Sandusky was quoted as giving a good description of the stamp. In his opinion this counterfeit printing was nearly perfect, with the color only slightly off. He pointed out that although these stamps had been perforated to look like the government's product, the perforations along the two edges were different than those that would be found on the legitimate government item.

Once these defendants were in the clutches of the government, it did not take long for some of them to conclude that cooperation, to at least some degree, was in their best interest. Charles Orr surrendered an additional 500,000 counterfeit stamps to the authorities. He then turned over the metal printing plates and the photo negative used to burn the plates. These plates had been laid out so that when each sheet of paper went through the press, the

36 Here we go again, a reference to a case I know nothing about.

impressions of 32 stamps would be printed.

The investigation would establish that the Dayton case was not simply an experiment in self-enterprise. Besides the primary offenders, another individual had come to the attention of the agents. This was Charles C. Schiehonzuber, who was the roommate of Mr. Kayser. When interviewed, he denied having any involvement with what had gone on. At the crime lab, however, after his fingerprints were compared to prints found on the recovered counterfeit stamps, 30 instances of his fingerprints were identified on the bogus items. He would also have a date in court.[37]

Besides Mr. Schiehonzuber, there were four other individuals who would be identified as at some point being involved with these counterfeit stamps. The United States Attorney ruled that he would decline to prosecute these men as he believed there was insufficient evidence that would tie them to this crime. It did, however, develop some interesting information.

One of these men had been selling the stamps out of his used furniture store. The story he would tell the investigators was chilling, but not original. The creation of these items did not come out of the minds of the people who the government had in custody. These stamps had been printed as part of a contract order. A representative from a large Cleveland business had requested they be printed. You can draw your own conclusions as to what this large Cleveland business was. Then at the last moment, the deal fell through. Unfortunately for the printers, they had already completed the order and now found themselves stuck with a large quantity of counterfeit stamps. Without any prepared distribution network, they wound up trying to sell the stamps on the street. Enter the police informant.

The investigation never did get to the people who had actually been behind this operation. Unlike TV, there is a big difference between what an investigator may know and what you can prove in court. The person who told the investigators the story behind the production of the stamps had also in no uncertain terms, informed them that he would not give that testimony in court. He had been visited by their representative. They had told him exactly what

37 For the wannabe counterfeiter a point that should be remembered: Gummed paper is just about the best medium known to man for retention of fingerprints.

would happen to him if he testified or caused any other problems. This sounds a lot like organized crime in operation, or a very bad Hollywood movie.

This case went to court in December of 1976, and one person who did testify was Charles Wiley Orr, the owner of the printing business used to produce the stamps. His testimony pretty well laid out what had happened.

Q: When did you first become involved in the scheme to counterfeit postage stamps?

A: The early part of January 1976.

Q: Who approached you?

A: A customer of Mr. Kayser's ... Charles Schiehonzuber... they had a buyer that wanted $1 million worth of U.S. postage stamps, 13-cent stamps ... I did the films, I did the plates, and I did the proofing. Samples were produced to where they could be given to the buyer to see if the quality was such that he would buy them.

Q: Who was present when the samples were produced?

A: Mr. Kayser ... they were given to Mr. Schiehonzuber, and he was to take them to the buyer ... (then) I went on vacation.

Q: What occurred in connection with these stamps when you came back?

A: They had been produced. The printing was done, the perforating was done, and they were doing the final cutting and packaging.

Q: What if anything, did Mr. Woodhouse do when he arrived?

A: He helped package and count.

Q: After the four of you split up, what happened to the stamps that had been printed?

A: The buyer did not want to buy them.*

*Thank God for small favors.

A small number of these stamps did not get distributed and used.

A: Mr. Woodhouse ... He had an individual that wanted to buy a small amount of stamps and at a later date could want to buy more.

Q: Did he tell you what kind of business this man was involved in?

A: Some type of direct mailing. I gave him one package which supposedly contained 899 stamps.

There was another amusing angle to the story. Early on, to establish if the stamps really were counterfeit, the informant had first taken a sample to a local stamp and coin dealer. When the stamp dealer checked the perforations he promptly identified these items as counterfeit. This stamp dealer also realized that he had a potential treasure in his hands and he kept a sample for himself. When he was later visited by agents, he would only surrender these treasures to the federal agents under threat of being prosecuted.

Ultimately, six individuals would be prosecuted in Dayton, Ohio. All of the defendants would either plead or be found guilty of counterfeiting offenses. Another positive point was that this case was a textbook example for interagency cooperation. By working together, these agents not only crushed a budding counterfeit operation, but they also uncovered the key to what was going on with very significant East Coast counterfeit operations. In the Dayton case file the following TWX message was discovered:

From: INC, Cincinnati, OH

To: Regional Chief, Chicago, IL

11-5-78

Case 613-48075-XMDO, Akron, OH

On September 29, 1976, Postal Clerk Herbert Soyk recovered 52 counterfeit 10-cent Jefferson Memorial stamps form Floyd Ray Tubbs, a customer at Stow Branch of the Akron, Ohio, Post Office. Immediate investigation by inspectors disclosed that Tubbs had received the counterfeit postage from Richard Holt, 4 Marion Street, Nesconset, NY. Tubbs advised that Holt provided the counterfeit postage to offset shipping expenses pursuant to a business transaction. The above information was submitted to the New York Division for appropriate investigation.

Continuing liaison between Inspector Hartman, Cleveland, Oh, and Inspector T. Sheehan, Westbury, NY, developed sufficient information to allow Postal Inspectors to obtain a search warrant for the business and residence of Richard Holt. This search warrant was executed by inspectors in the New York Division on November 4, 1976, and led to the recovery of 155,000 counterfeit 10-cent Jefferson Memorial postage stamps $15,500 in value, counterfeit currency (one $1,000 note) and unlicensed automatic weapons. Holt is currently a subject of investigation by the ATF and Secret Service, and is believed to have organized crime connections. He is expected to surrender to Postal Inspectors on the afternoon of November 5 ...

Notes in the file stated that the criminal complaint against Richard T. Holt was dismissed because it was felt the government was never able to establish on his part the elements of knowledge or criminal intent. Assistant U.S. Attorney Susan Sheperd stated that it would be incumbent upon the government to prove that Mr. Holt knowingly and willfully possessed and used the counterfeit stamps that the agents had seized. In her view, the search of Holt's business and residence had been premature and criminality had not been established by the agents.

Other information presented a slightly different impression. It indicated the government believed that Holt could be turned into a "cooperative witness" (snitch). By letting Holt walk, the Federal Strike Force may have been simply trying to trade up. He had information the government wanted. In the world of federal prosecution and the war against the Mafia, this is how the Mob was finally taken apart. One moral of this story could be, if you are going to get involved in criminal activity, have somebody available you can trade away when the agents kick in your door.[38]

The arrest of Holt was significant. It was directly the result of information coming out of the Dayton case. With the arrest of Holt, 155,225 counterfeit 10-cent Jefferson Memorial stamps (Scott #1510) were seized along with eight unregistered handguns and at least one

38 This also points out the danger of who you may be associating with. I once had an individual I knew try to give me up to ATF and Customs in Cleveland. Could have been a problem except one of the agents knew me from working undercover.

machine gun. Even though they had been miserably printed, what made the stamps found in Holt's possession scary, was they had been packaged to look exactly like they had been shipped from the Bureau of Engraving and Printing. Each package contained 100 sheets of stamps wrapped in kraft paper with the upper right corner cut out to allow a glimpse of the stamps. Each "deck" of stamps had a buff-colored cover sheet printed in imitation of the "NOTICE" inserted with each legitimate stamp package that came out of the "BEP."

It has always been my suspicion that these counterfeits had been designed to be inserted into postal accountability. Imagine that these bogus "decks" could be introduced into a large Post Office stamp stock or better yet into the Stamp Storage Repository at Kansas City.[39] Actually, you did not have to go that far afield. If we are dealing with organized crime, you can always find a compliant postal employee who for one reason or another you can talk into exchanging his stamps for yours. If he is really self-enterprising, all he has to do is slide the bogus stamps into the office accountability and walk off with an offsetting amount of cash or authentic stamps.

39 Security at the repository was not foolproof. A surprise audit was conducted in the 1990s. Imagine the inspector's surprise when it was discovered that $500,000 in stamps were missing. The boxes were there, but the contents had been removed. Then the boxes had been closed again and resealed. This was a crime which to the best of my knowledge never was solved.

5

Things Came Together

In 1977 I was back in external crimes, making undercover check and credit card buys. Then, one day my boss called me in and asked me to go over to the Secret Service office. They had an informant report that counterfeit stamps were again available in Chicago. Relations at the moment were strained between our agencies, and the thought was that I might be able to smooth things out. I had a history of working well with the Secret Service both in Texas and in Chicago. Besides that, I had some small knowledge of stamps and how they were produced. Thus began an adventure that would play a large role in my work in the Inspection Service.

A productive meeting occurred and it was agreed that both agencies would work together. I was teamed up with Special Agent Frank Forgione and for the next two years I virtually took up residence with the Secret Service counterfeit division. First in the investigation of this case, and then in its prosecution, Frank and I bumped into many technical and historical questions. What I would soon discover is that the Treasury Department maintains voluminous records, whereas the Post Office simply maintained little or no institutional memory. At least this was so where stamp counterfeiting was concerned.

In this case a different approach would be called for than what the inspectors had been forced to do with the crossed-flag investigation. First and foremost, we had a relatively good idea (courtesy of an informant) who the primary distributors were. This was a starting point that enabled us to jump over all the preliminary steps the inspectors had been forced to go through in the earlier case. Working with our informant, a series of stamp buys were made. Eventually this enabled us to move an agent in as a person who wanted to purchase a large quantity of counterfeit stamps. Our idea was not necessarily to soak up all the counterfeit stamps available on the street. Rather, the target was to identify the press and if possible, get it running again.

The informant identified the stamp being printed as the 13-

cent Kennedy, and he soon supplied copies for our examination. Besides being an offset printing, for the Post Office, the one glaring identification point was that once again it lacked phosphor tagging. This meant that in mail processing these items should be kicked out by the facer/cancellers. With the help of a few inspectors, we were able to examine the rejects and a number of counterfeits were pulled out of the mail stream.

It had been decided in the initial stages we would just note who the mailers were and let the mail go through for delivery. This generated an in-house argument in the Inspection Service as to whether recording such information would constitute a mail cover or not. From an investigative standpoint our response was simple. Bite me, we are going to do it. At this time we were not going to confront the mailers. Our argument was simple: We are trying to get the people who made the stamps, not those who were simply selling or using them.

This approach worked, and step-by-step the individuals involved were identified. Affectionately we soon dubbed the group the "Over The Hill Gang." The nickname was appropriate. A number of these players were pushing senior citizen status and we documented they had a long history with organized crime. The men were all colorful characters, mostly worker bees who never quite hit the big time. If not full-fledged members of the "Outfit," these folks had, at the very least, been existing on the periphery and moved freely in those circles. One of them would later relate how in his youth he had the distinction of being Al Capone's driver.

The pieces of this investigation actually came together fairly rapidly. This was mostly from the efforts of the Secret Service. Through monitored conversations with sellers, it was soon established that the stamps we were finding in Illinois and Indiana had been printed in Chicago. Time and again we were told that only a single press run had occurred and then everything had been shut down. This frustrated our attempts to get them to fire up the press again so a larger quantity of stamps could be produced.[40] Still, through undercover stamp buys, identifying the perforator, and the gummed

40 The more counterfeit currency or stamps you can wheel into a courtroom, the more serious the offense will be viewed by the judge. It also makes your prosecution a lot easier when you can say, "And here judge is the printing press."

paper used, accompanied with very selective mailer interviews, the case was worked back from street-level users and sellers up to the persons who actually manufactured the stamps. Eventually we came to the end of the line and it was time to take the criminals down.

On May 9, 1977, we arrested Calogero Coppola for the sale of 5,000 counterfeit stamps, and $13,000 in counterfeit currency to an undercover Secret Service agent. On November 16, he would enter a guilty plea and on January 20, 1978, be sentenced to two years in custody to be followed by three years of probation.

On May 16, 1977, Anthony Rainone was arrested for the sale of 5,000 counterfeit stamps to an undercover agent. In a three-day trial, Rainone was found guilty of the sale and possession of counterfeit stamps. On April 28, 1978, he was sentenced to 15 months custody of the attorney general. Information would subsequently be developed that identified Rainone as the person responsible for the transportation of a large quantity of these counterfeit stamps from Chicago to Providence, Rhode Island and other eastern locations.

On November 16, 1977, Virgil Rutili was arrested for the sale of 60,000 counterfeit stamps to an undercover agent. In developing this investigation, it was determined that Virgil Rutili was the primary distributor. He was one step removed from the printing of the stamps. Rutili's stamp source was identified as Anthony Vecelli.

As we moved through the players, besides surveillance and following various individuals around, consensual electronic surveillance had been authorized and was utilized in both face-to-face, and in monitored conversations. It was firmly established Anthony Vecelli was the person who had the primary responsibility for distribution of the counterfeits from the printing press to the street.

Once again, when we checked the records for printing equipment sales, it paid dividends. Purchase records showed that one round-hole Rosback perforating machine had been acquired by Lawrence Vodvarka. He was the owner and operator of B&A Printing. It was established that after its sale, this machine had been picked up by Anthony Vecelli. Reviewing Secret Service records, it was found that back in 1938, Anthony Vecelli had been identified with Lawrence Vodvarka's father for distribution of counterfeit currency. When the items recovered in undercover buys were treated for fingerprints, five separate instances were found of Lawrence Vodvarka's fingerprints on said stamps.

On June 8, 1978, a superseding indictment was returned by a Special Chicago Grand Jury. It charged Virgil Rutili, Anthony Vecelli and Lawrence Vodvarka with violating Title 18 United States Code, Section 501 (Manufacturing and Distribution), and 371 (Conspiracy) to counterfeit United States Postage Stamps. Lawrence Vodvarka was taken into custody on June 19, 1978.

With his court date rolling around, Anthony Vecelli failed to appear and he was declared a federal fugitive. The trial of Virgil Rutili, Lawrence Vodvarka and Anthony Vecelli was again scheduled for August 7, 1978. As the defendants in this case had been identified as having an organized crime background, the prosecution of the case was turned over to an attorney from the Chicago Organized Crime Strike Force. All of the defendants would be successfully prosecuted and convicted on these offenses.

Before it was over, this case had taken more than two years out of my life. Any time you spend that amount of time on any one case and in such close contact with your targets, you develop some degree of relationship with those you are dealing with. We spent many days and nights both listening to their conversations and following them around. At one point Anthony Rainone spotted our tail, and then took us on a tour of southern Illinois. Later Anthony and agents would sit around laughing about it. He would also regale us with his memories of the early days in the "Chicago Outfit."

Mostly Rainone was entertaining. He told one tale about the Christmas he had enjoyed when Sinatra was featured at a show Sam Giancana put on for his associates. He and Rutili would joke about how they honed their printing skills while guests of the federal government at Sandstone, Minnesota. This job skill turned out to be handy when it came time to print the Kennedy stamps. As they related events, the individual who normally handled the Mob's plate and printing projects was no longer available.[41] Then, one day Vecelli gave me some additional food for thought.

It turned out this was not their first rodeo. "You know,

41 This may be a reference to an individual identified as "da Vinci" in Jason Kersten's book, "The Art of Making Money."

this is not the first time we did stamps." He related how he and his colleagues began targeting postage stamps back in the 1960s. Apparently, they had printed and distributed the then current 5-cent stamp (Washington, Scott #1213, issued November 23, 1962). As he remembered the event, millions of these stamps were printed and distributed. Later I would conclude this may have been the source of the Detroit counterfeit printing plate previously mentioned as occurring in July of 1967.

As Rainone went on to describe this and other enterprises, he claimed the Washington stamp operation was set up and run by Joseph Anthony LaBarbara. "You know LaBarbara. It was at his house, the New York House where the bosses met in Appalachia." He was referring to the Appalachian, New York conference in 1962, where all the bosses in organized crime had gathered for a secret meeting to divide up criminal activity in the United States. This little get together was discovered by a "nosy" State Patrol officer who took notice of all the flashy cars with out-of-state license plates. The raid that ensued caused a number of heavyset and dapperly dressed men to flee through the woods in their expensive suits and shoes. The result may have been comical, but it got the notice of the media, and made self-evident that yes there was this thing called organized crime in the United States. It even contributed to forcing J. Edgar Hoover to finally acknowledge that this criminal organization did exist in this country.[42]

One of the more memorable events in this case occurred during one of the first undercover stamp buys. This meeting had taken place at a well-known (both for its food and its connections) Italian eatery on Chicago's West Side. An undercover agent wearing a wire was negotiating the purchase of a package of stamps. They were occupying a table off to the side. Imagine the agent's surprise, if not joy, when the adjacent table was suddenly occupied by no less than Anthony "Big Tuna" Accardo. At that time, Tony was the reputed number two man in the Chicago Outfit. In reality, years later it would be discovered that in Chicago, Tony was really the power behind the

42 Of course these same folks were providing Hoover with lodging while catering to his interest in horse racing in both Miami and Sarasota each year. Strange how that worked.

throne. He was the person who pulled the criminal strings.

There is a very good reason why the federal government seldom loses when they bring a case to trial. Before your case even sees a U.S. attorney, the crime and those who perpetrated it have been very thoroughly investigated. An arrest is just the beginning, not the end of the story. If there are any loose ends they are tied up in your court preparation.

One loose end in our Kennedy case was the perforator. The purchase of a perforator had been documented. The next step was matching the machine in question to the one that had been used on the stamps we had recovered. The final nail in the defendant's coffin was when fingerprints found on the counterfeit stamps were positively matched with those of the defendant's. That was the key to Lawrence Vodvarka's identification and subsequent prosecution. When his fingerprints were identified on the stamps, by inference he was identified as the printer. He had a significant prior criminal history with arrests for counterfeiting and his reported connections with organized crime. When the trial took place, it was a slam dunk for the prosecution.

At some point in Chicago while investigating counterfeit stamps, they became a personal obsession. Part of my curiosity grew out of trial preparation, but also it was founded on my being a stamp collector. For trial preparation I did not want some bright defense attorney asking questions I did not have any answers to. To tie up loose ends in the case, and also to address my personal curiosity, I began to dig into just how much of this activity had gone on in the past. When I began to explore the history, it was like pulling on a loose string in a sweater. The history began to unravel, and the cases just kept going on and on.

In Chicago we had recovered approximately 120,000 counterfeit stamps. Other seizures occurred in Rockford, Illinois and in Indiana. Still, information had been developed in electronic monitoring that showed that distribution had taken place in other parts of the country. This apparently was an established procedure with these folks. "Alert" notifications were sent out to other divisions and X-case requests to follow up on leads were sent to specific locations. It was not long before responses came back.

In Providence, Rhode Island, Postal Inspector T.E. Maher

reported that he had recovered 10,000 stamps. Inspector Maher identified Albert E. Parente as a major East Coast distributor. He was arrested on September 29, 1977, and charged with nine counts of possession and sale of counterfeit stamps. On April 4, 1978, Parente would be convicted on those charges.

In Inspector Maher's case, a confidential informant provided him information that counterfeit Kennedy stamps were available and being used in the Providence, Rhode Island area. On the night of September 21, 1977, postal inspectors took a look at the collection mail. They found counterfeit stamps. Teaming up with the Secret Service they served six search warrants on businesses in the Rhode Island area. This is where the 10,000 stamps came from that Inspector Maher would use in the prosecution of Parente.

Providence had apparently developed into a major counterfeit distribution hub for the Northeast. In following the trail of stamps associated with Providence, it soon became apparent to the inspectors that they were dealing not simply with counterfeit stamps from Chicago. Yes, there was the Chicago stamp, but then it appears they also tripped over two other presses, one located in Boston and another in New York City. Boston can be identified as the location of one press, as approximately 13 million unfinished stamps were found floating in the Boston Harbor. The stamps in the Boston Harbor were copies of the Liberty Bell. These stamps appeared to be a step-repeat printing where a single image was copied over and over. In step-repeat printing the same identification characteristics (or errors) will appear on each and every stamp. Another step-repeat reproduction associated with Boston was a copy of the Kennedy stamp. On the Boston Kennedy, the error noted on each stamp was a faint line directly above the cent mark.

The press believed to be located in the New York City area appeared to be half-tone screen printing. Now mind you, a press capable of doing half-tone screen printing is not something you generally find in someone's basement. This is a type of printing that is normally used for multi-colored illustrations similar to colored prints you find in an upscale magazine. Half-tone screen printing is easily identified. If you put the colored image under magnification your image will appear as a series of small dots.

When I began to look into what had been going on, I discovered that a whole series of stamps could be identified in the Northeast, printed using half-tone screen. This was a press that appeared to have been in operation for many years. Some of the stamps printed were the 10-cent Jefferson Memorial, 13-cent red airmail (Scott #C79), 13-cent Kennedy, and another version of the 13-cent Liberty Bell.

After I was informed of Inspector Maher's investigation, I began to seriously dig into and review everything I could find on East Coast operations. I soon concluded that for some time an absolute rat's nest of counterfeiting activity had been occurring. This would only be reinforced when I began to put together the current cases with what had occurred in the past.

Not going too far back, at Foster, Rhode Island, in November of 1976, $3,000 in counterfeit 13-cent Liberty Bell stamps were found next to the body of Anthony Paraziale. Both Paraziale and the stamps were in the front seat of his station wagon. The cause of his death would be listed as a shotgun blast to his head. Somebody had obviously been sending a message to someone. Police intelligence files would identify Paraziale as being an associate of organized crime. He was listed as a suspected fence, and a well-known gambler. Additional informant information came in that indicated that Paraziale's murder was directly related to his continued dealing with the counterfeit stamps. It was speculated that with the sudden heat coming down from federal agents, at least for the moment, somebody in authority had pulled out of the counterfeit stamp business.

If a message was being transmitted, the thought was it had been received. It was shortly after Paraziale's killing that the Boston inspectors would report the discovery of bundles of 13- cent Liberty Bells floating in the Boston Bay. Other than being wet, the stamps appeared to have come right off of the printing press. Indicating that the source of the stamps was a large and probably professional printing shop, these stamp sheets were printed with 400 stamps per sheet in the format of four panes of 100 stamps each. These stamp sheets had not yet been either cut into individual panes or perforated. The Boston Liberty Bell counterfeit when found in circulation was perforated on all four sides.

Then a call came in from Miami requesting assistance. Miami

reported they had a counterfeit Kennedy stamp down there that they suspected came from Chicago. In the mail processing, Kennedy stamps were being rejected by the cancelling machines. When examined, those stamps were identified as being the product of step- repeat printing, and immediately associated with the Boston press, not Chicago. In Miami the counterfeits were being used by a business sending out fundraising solicitation requests reportedly for the Fraternal Order of Police. Organized crime had long ago infiltrated the mail preparation business, as well as fundraising charity solicitations so this was a ready market for fraudulent postage. It was also suspected that the entire operation was possibly a straight-forward mail fraud. Ultimately, the investigation would again lead back to the Northeast.

Shortly after "Spurious Stamps" was published in 1996, another connection to Florida was found. Again it related to the step-repeat 13-cent Boston Liberty Bell. A letter had been sent to William Hatton who had written about this counterfeit stamp in *Linn's Stamp News.* The letter was authored by William Bomer of the U.S. Cancellation Club.

Bomer had attended the spring meeting of the Society of Philatelic Americans down in Florida when he made an unusual discovery. William Boggs of the New England Stamp Company had moved his business from Boston down to Naples, Florida in the mid 1970s. In Florida he continued to work the show circuit, as well as his walk-in stamp store in Naples, Florida. As Bomer was walking around the show floor way in the back he observed some unusual activity.

There in the back was Kenneth Brown, Boggs' trusted assistant, and Judy the office secretary. They were sitting at a back table sorting through two large apple type boxes that gave every appearance of containing commonly used stamps. Wondering what they were doing, Bomer inquired why they would be wasting their time on such mundane material. The casual reply he got back was that "it was just simply something to do." Still he wondered, and as the show went on all weekend long, Boggs noted that Bill, Ken, and Judy were continually digging through those boxes of common stamps that appeared to have little, if any, value.

When the show was over Bomer got together with Boggs, and his curiosity drove him to pin Boggs down. After lubricating him with a couple of drinks, the true story finally came out of Boggs:

"You are aware that the New England Stamp Shop has for a number of years done a large business in selected postal history – want lists – items sent out on approval.... You may recall we always enclosed a good quality brown Kraft envelope with postage attached to encourage prompt returns. For years when these envelopes were returned we simply clipped the used stamps from our returned manila envelopes and tossed them into a large box under the mail table."

Bill's recollection was that one day he had taken in trade several thousand dollars worth of mint stamp sheets at a significant discount. This is not something that is unusual in the stamp trade business. After he had taken these stamps in trade, Bill used them on his inserted mailing envelopes he was sending out to his clients. Almost four years after these stamps had been acquired and had been used in his mailings, it was brought to his attention that something was wrong with these stamps.

The stamp in question was the 13-cent Liberty Bell. What Boggs' customer had noted was that the stamps on the return envelope had perforations on all four sides. The Liberty Bell stamp issued by the government had only been issued in either coil or booklet form. The stamps Boggs had been using were obviously counterfeits meant to defraud the government. The next development was several months later when Ken Brown, his assistant, remembered the boxes of clipped used stamps they had accumulated under the counter.

When the Port Charlotte stamp show was going on, things were slow. Realizing they had something of value in those counterfeit items, they decided to call Judy, the secretary, back in Naples. They asked her to close up the shop and bring those boxes down to the show. To occupy their time they figured they could check to see if any of those bogus stamps might have been returned. In the first 30 minutes they found six or eight examples. By the time the show was over, they had accumulated enough of those items to fill a large manila-sized legal envelope.

Boggs told Mr. Bomer that he thought he had received the bogus stamps from someone who came from the Midwest. The way counterfeit stamps were going back and forth between the East Coast and the Midwest made that possible, but I find that very questionable.

The New England Stamp Company was located in Boston, which I strongly believe was the location of the press. Considering who I suspect was involved in producing these stamps, if I was Boggs, I am not sure I would want to remember who the source of those counterfeit stamps was either.

There was kind of a standing joke in the Inspection Service about the Secret Service and organized crime when counterfeit stamps were encountered. The knee-jerk reaction was to exclaim, "Ah ha - organized crime, i.e. La Cosa Nostra." Frequently that was true, but when Boston was the location this identification had to be questioned. In Boston, crime was anything but organized. It was a study in ethnic diversity.

With all the counterfeit stamps that apparently were floating around in the Northeast, from an investigative standpoint, there was little if any coordination going on. With both the counterfeit Kennedy and the Liberty Bell stamps, inspectors in different divisions were investigating the same counterfeit stamps. When I began to look into those investigations and tie them together, the impression I drew was that there was little if any coordination going on. This was not a criticism of either the inspectors, or for that matter their administrators. It simply was the way each administrative division in the Inspection Service was structured and how we functioned.

The same degree of frustration was discovered when I attempted to look into Postal and Inspection Service record keeping. This has probably been the Achilles heel of the Inspections Service in combating counterfeit postage. When I attempted to get information on either current or prior stamp investigations, I discovered there were few if any historical files or documentation of old cases. This was not the result of some nefarious plan, but simply the result of administrators not recognizing that counterfeiting is a problem that needed to be systematically attacked. You cannot treat counterfeiting like a standard localized criminal investigation. History needs to be remembered and records maintained of who these people are and what they had done. As it was, and unfortunately still is, every time an inspector picks up a stamp investigation, he or she literally has to reinvent the wheel.

It was the discovery that there was a dearth of official records that had driven me to begin my own personal research. This would involve contacting individual inspectors to find out what they had or were working on, and then digging into news files and court records. As the pieces of these cases came together, the more it was evident that a record of this activity had to be created.

One story I stumbled upon was a minor affair involving the 15-cent Oliver Wendell Holmes. This was neither a Secret Service nor a Postal Inspector investigation and like many counterfeiting cases, it seemed to come out of left field. The FBI broke this case and my immediate reaction was to question what they had been doing playing in either our, or the Secret Service sandbox. Actually it was a very well-executed and appropriate investigation for the FBI.

The impression I had was that neither the Secret Service nor the postal inspectors knew anything about this investigation until they heard about it in the news. In Philadelphia, on the night of November 27, 1980, agents arrested George Capwell and James Dagney. The news reported that agents had raided the Conestoga Press located at 520 Knorr Street. At that location agents had found eight sheets of counterfeit 15 postage stamps.

Most likely the immediate response of anyone who heard this report would have been – you have got to be kidding (eight sheets of stamps?). Actually, the case was slightly more involved than that. Special Agent John Kundts was the lead agent, and when he went to the Knorr Street address he was not looking for stamps. When asked to explain what had gone on, his response was that these arrests were the result of a two-month investigation by the Bureau. The Comptroller and Treasurer of the Southeastern Pennsylvania Transportation Authority (SEPTA) had contacted the Bureau and requested their assistance. For some time, the Transportation Authority had suspected they were losing an estimated $1 million per month as the result of someone producing and then selling bogus monthly train passes.

A number of suspect train passes had been accumulated by the Transportation Authority. These were turned over to Special Agent Kundts, and he promptly submitted them to the Bureau's crime lab. Not surprisingly the lab determined that, yes, the suspected items were in fact counterfeit. Then the lab went a step further. They identified that both the genuine and the counterfeit train passes had been printed on the same unique paper. Just like our currency, the distribution of this paper was very tightly controlled and monitored.

With this information, it did not take long for James M. Dagney to be identified as a purchaser. Not only that, he had paid for the paper with checks drawn on the Conestoga Press. Using surveillance, discreet interviews, and wire taps, FBI agents gathered adequate information that would justify and support the issuance of a search warrant. The affidavit that Agent Kundts filed to support this search warrant was actually 30 pages in length.[43] Agent Kundts was either very wordy, or very thorough in the investigation he had put together.

When the search was executed the Bureau's agents were not disappointed. They found the bogus TransPasses they were looking for. Then they also found Delaware River Port Authority Bridge tickets, Department of Motor Vehicle Inspection Service Tickets, and finally the eight sheets of counterfeit stamps. The one thing that was missing was the plates used to print all of the aforementioned. As for the stamps, their printing appeared to be only at an experimental stage. Each of the eight sheets was in a slightly different shade of color showing that the printer was still experimenting and trying to get an exact stamp color match to the government's product. None of the printed sheets had yet to be perforated.

On May 19, 1981, George Capewell entered a guilty plea to the 13-count indictment lodged against him. He had been charged with 11 counts of mail fraud and just one count of counterfeiting and an additional one of conspiracy. James Dagney, bless his soul, elected to go to trial. The U.S. Attorney requested that Document Analyst R. W. French of the Postal Inspections Service Crime Laboratory testify as to the counterfeit nature of the stamps found.

Now, you may be wondering why Capewell had been charged with mail fraud. Actually, from a prosecution standpoint, mail fraud is one of the greatest laws ever passed. The heart of the statute is "causing the mail to be used in the furtherance or commission of an offense," or as one defense attorney described it – "Walking by a mailbox with evil intent." When you think about it, it is virtually

43 My philosophy was always "The less said the better." I don't think I ever filed an affidavit that was longer than five pages.

impossible to commit any kind of sophisticated criminal endeavor without causing someone somewhere to put something in the mail.

When the case against Dagney went to trial, the press found great amusement, not necessarily with the crime, but with the perpetrator himself. One newspaper, the Philadelphia Daily News, captured the spirit of the event. They described the offender as "a beer drinking man who felt that working for a living was foolish." This master criminal was a 40-year-old, unemployed truck driver who carried a can of beer everywhere he went. Apparently unemployed, he still seemed to get along quite well financially. According to the paper:

> While on welfare, he plunked down $20,000 in bank certificates of deposit. ... Out of work for nearly two years, he put $6,000 down on a house in Drexel Hill last year, and later pulled $66,540 in cash out of a paper bag to close the deal. He also paid $10,000 cash for a car.

Dagney really made no attempt to stay under the radar, and his lifestyle had not gone unnoticed by just about anyone he encountered. Where he banked, employees wondered where someone on food stamps would get the sacks of small bills that he was always exchanging for larger bills. The Assistant U.S. Attorney who prosecuted this case had an answer. He described to the court Dagney's source of income as "paper gold."

Originally, Dagney had been printing his counterfeit documents in his own basement. Then, when his printing press broke down, he approached Capewell and talked him into taking over the printing in this enterprise. Under arrest, Capewell saw the error of his ways, and would testify as a government witness. He acknowledged that, yes, he had been the printer. He related how Dagney had given him $10,000 to set up a new printing operation in his print shop. He explained how in their agreement he would be paid $1,000 each month for the SEPTA TransPasses he would produce.

In court, agents testified that frequently Dagney would be observed walking out of the print shop with a beer in one hand and a bag of TransPasses in the other. On the street he would then sell these items for 50 percent of their face value. It can easily be imagined that if this counterfeiting operation had gone on much longer their next target would have been postage stamps. Most likely he would have merchandised them the same way he had the TransPasses, selling them door-to-door on the street.

One might suspect that targeting something as common as a TransPass would be an insignificant crime, but it was not. In 1980, SEPTA reported they had lost more than $2.5 million in revenue to counterfeiting activity. Because operations of the Transportation Authority were underwritten by the U.S. taxpayer, it was thus under the authority of the U.S. Transportation Department. This was the justification used to request federal intervention and assistance.

In return for Mr. Capewell's cooperation and testimony in court, he was sentenced to six months work release with additional three years' probation and a $5,000 fine. With Dagney, the court was less generous. He was sentenced to three years in custody to be followed by three years' probation and a $20,000 fine.

Thanks to the FBI, this time the Post Office just may have dodged a bullet.

Then They Hit the Target – St. Louis 1982

One day in Chicago I was having coffee with Inspector T.J. Smith from the St. Louis division.

I do not remember exactly when this occurred, but T.J. made the offhand comment that down in St. Louis he was working on a counterfeit case. I had no idea what he had gotten into, but I asked him to keep me posted. This is what happened.

On August 5, 1982, four men were arrested in St. Louis, Mo., and charged with manufacturing counterfeit stamps. The items duplicated were described as denominations of 5, 20, and 37 cents. Agents seized the plates and negatives and $3,265 in counterfeit stamps. Special Agent Jay Foushee of the Secret Service commented: "Stamp counterfeiting is a rare type of thing, but if there wasn't a market for them, they wouldn't have been making them."[44]

Sounds real simple – right? The story got about three inches of ink in the paper. This did not even scratch the surface of what was

44 It is because of such statements that I began to write about stamp counterfeiting. Counterfeiting is many things, but rare it is not.

an incredibly important story. To tell what transpired I am going to excerpt some of the case reports that were sent to me. It will also give a bird's eye view of how this case was put together. Sometimes you have no idea where following the string will take you.

This story really began on February 25, 1982, when St. Louis County Police Officer Thomas L. Robinson called the postal inspectors. Officer Robinson had been working undercover with the Drug Enforcement Task Force. In the course of his work, he had developed a relationship with an informant who had presented him with something out of his standard area of expertise. Robinson had recruited this informant the way most informants are recruited. He had been involved in a large drug operation. Facing arrest, he was given a simple choice: You can work your case off by supplying information to the officer on criminal activity in the St. Louis area, or plan on going directly to jail. When he called, the question Officer Robinson asked the postal inspectors was if they might be interested in a postage counterfeiting operation he had just found out about.

The tale his informant had spun was that he had been approached by a female acquaintance who apparently had been offered $10,000 by a third party to locate a printer who could make counterfeit stamps. Not knowing any printers herself, this woman had told the informant that if he could come up with a good printer she would share the $10,000 with him. The first thing Robinson had done was try to establish the reliability of this information. He ran a name check on the woman and determined that although she herself had no criminal record, her family was an entirely different story. They were identified as being connected with organized crime factions in the St. Louis area.

Robinson immediately got the attention of the local inspectors, and they jumped on the opportunity to work with the officer and his informant. The St. Louis division was under the jurisdiction of the Inspection Service Central Region and if there was any location that was conscious of postal counterfeits it was in the Midwest. The first step was setting up a meeting between the informant, his female friend, and the mysterious third party who was looking for a printer.

This was just a preliminary meeting with the goal of eventually inserting a third party (an agent) into the mix. This appeared to go down without any problems, and immediately after the meeting, the informant was reeled in and debriefed. He brought in new information that got everyone's attention. He had been told there was a lot of money to be made with counterfeit stamps and little danger of discovery. It appeared that the people doing this already had the paper and supplies and all they needed was a good printer. The informant had been told that this was going to be an ongoing operation and the printer could expect to earn from $20,000 to $25,000 every couple of weeks for his efforts.

What was more disturbing was that the informant had been told that the counterfeiting activity of this group had been going on for a number of years. Now, they needed a new printer as the individual who had been doing their work had recently died. None of the stamps would be sold in the St. Louis area. Apparently, on a regular basis stamps produced in St. Louis had been distributed across the country. This was a very big and very profitable operation.[45]

Based on the information that had been developed, Postal Inspectors Stinson and T.J. Smith brought in Special Agent William Noonan of the Secret Service. Now with the Secret Service working with them they set up another meeting with this third party. The purpose of this get together was to introduce an agent into the mix who was playing the role of a low-level St. Louis criminal who just happened to have a cousin in the printing business. Again, this individual repeated everything he had previously told the informant. Only this time it was recorded.

Again this person was dropping some very strong hints that he was "representing some big people." He emphasized that they had been in the stamp business for several years and the people he represented wanted approximately $3,000,000 worth of bogus stamps printed each year. As they parted he agreed that when he got the approval of those he reported to, he would give the undercover agent $5,000 to cover any expenses incurred to set up the printing operation.

Establishing the credibility of their informant and to support

45 The names of both the female and the third party have not been used: First of all, I do not wish to be sued, and secondly, I do not want my car to blow up some morning. This was also another reference to the regular printer no longer being available. It is my suspicion this is actually my old friend from Chicago who called me one night and visited. Possibly he also went by the name of Di Vinci.

any case that could be developed, the informant was given a polygraph examination that he passed with flying colors. The next step was to identify who the players were. They ran background checks on the person they had met with and it was verified this person had access to, if not directly connected with, several high-ranking organized crime figures operating in the St. Louis area. The agents concluded that thanks to Officer Robinson the government had stumbled across a very significant criminal operation. Now all they had to do was wrap it up.

One thing you soon learn when dealing with criminals is they do not have what you would call a high reliability index. The agents wanted to push this case along, yet suddenly the person they were dealing with dropped out of sight. It was a month later before any follow-up meeting could be arranged. Pressed about what was going on, he gave the excuse he had been having a problem contacting his people. He stated that they needed to come up with the front money before they could get things going. In an attempt to keep himself relevant, the informant presses about himself becoming a distributor. In no uncertain terms he was told that they already had a distribution system in place, and what they printed would not be distributed or sold in the St. Louis area.

In most Inspection Service cases, the first the United States Attorney hears about your investigation is when you walk in his door with someone already in cuffs, you caught him in the act, or you are dropping a U.S. Attorney prosecution letter on his desk. The exception to this is complex or major prosecutions where your U.S. Attorney wants to be involved from the get go. That bell had been rung on a number of levels. First, this was an organized crime case, and secondly, electronic surveillance was going to be utilized. Both required very active Justice Department involvement.

When time went by and things appeared to be stalled, Assistant U.S. Attorney Richard L. Poehling decided to light his own fire. He told the agents that he was tired of being jacked around and he decided the informant maybe needed a little motivation. He told the agents to tell the informant that because he had not produced results, the U.S. Attorney's office was going to indict him on his prior drug distribution charges and arrest him. When you are facing imminent arrest and prosecution, this does have the tendency to concentrate your attention.

As a general rule, U.S. Attorneys do not make idle threats. On May 19, he had the informant arrested. Now in jail, the informant told the agents that he would do everything possible to move things along. Now with his attention focused, after he posted a $50,000 surety bond, he was again put on the street. The informant really was trying, but all of his efforts were frustrated. He reported that he had the feeling that something was wrong and his contact now appeared to be avoiding him. There could have been a number of reasons this would occur; they may have found their printer already, or just maybe, they no longer trusted him. As any criminal with half a brain knows, if you were arrested, and are now suddenly back on the street, a natural question is to wonder why. Have you cut a deal?

Then it appeared there could be another reason. John Vitale, the reputed head of organized crime in St. Louis, had died. This had caused a vacuum at the top, and an immediate drop in organized "Mob" activity. Until things could be sorted out, and a new boss installed, everything was up in the air. Nobody wanted to do anything that the new boss might take exception to. Then suddenly other events would intervene.

The best way to describe what occurred is to use some of the actual communications that went on:

From New York to all Divisions:

The New York Robbery/Burglary team was contacted on 07/19/82 by a confidential informant who stated he could arrange the purchase of $100,000 worth of stolen U.S. postage. The CI provided samples of 18-cent George Mason, 20-cent Ralph Bunche, and 02-cent Freedom to Speak Out stamps (three stamps of each denomination). The Northeast Region crime lab examined the samples and determined the 18-cent and 20-cent are counterfeit while the 02-cent samples are genuine.

U.S. Secret Service New York office was contacted and a plan for a buy-bust was developed with the counterfeit squad. On 07/20/82 the CI was requested to obtain whole sheet samples of the stamps. The second group of samples were 18-cent George Mason, 37-cent Robert Milkan and "C" stamps. The lab found all to be counterfeit.

A "buy" was arranged for 07/27/82. A task force of U.S.S.S. agents and postal inspectors conducted a surveillance of the stamp source which began in midtown Manhattan and ended in Bayonne, NJ that evening. Three individuals were arrested and approximately $200,000 worth of counterfeit postage was recovered. Those arrested were: Percival "Percy" Longmore DOB 12/28/49, Elias "Mo" Mahanna, DOB 07/21/33, Anthony "Junior" Serpe, DOB 08/21/34.

The undercover agents first met Longmore who was serving as a "Go-between." Longmore took the agents to Mahanna who was controlling the counterfeit postage. Mahanna then took the agents to Serpe who was holding the postage for Mahanna. The postage was recovered from the trunk of one of the vehicles, a dumpster where some of the postage was stashed, and a suitcase in Serpe's apartment pursuant to a consent search.

A consent search was also conducted at Janis International Sales, Inc., 140 W. 36 St., NY, NY, Mahanna's place of business. Letters linking Mahanna to the printing of U.S. postage as well as evidence of a plan to operate stamp vending machines were found.

Mahanna admitted receiving these stamps from Al Castaldi in St. Louis, Mo. A telephone call was placed to Castaldi by Mahanna and the conversation monitored. Mahanna requested more stamps and Castaldi advised he could deliver but the press was disassembled. He stated it would take three to four days to be operational.

The three individuals arrested are being arraigned in the District of New Jersey today. Mahanna will continue to cooperate. St. Louis Division has been contacted.

It was evident the New York area had been a primary destination for stamps being printed in St. Louis. It is also evident this was not a new market. Still, the events in New York would be used to jump start the stalled investigation in St. Louis. Picking things up, the Secret Service in St. Louis determined Castaldi was one of three "middle men" who had been looking for a new printer. The other individuals identified were Jack Fink, DOB 11-25-14 and Mike Saputo, DOB 04-27-30. In monitored telephone conversations, the Secret Service had Mahanna in New York place an order with Castaldi for the purchase of $250,000 worth of counterfeit stamps. The price to be paid on delivery was $25,000. It was agreed the items would be supplied as soon as Castaldi could arrange for a new printing.

Under surveillance Castaldi subsequently contacted one Mr. M.A Saunders, DOB 02-25-28 who was the owner of Saunders Printing Company, 789 South Highway 67, Florisant, Mo. Apparently arrangements for the printing had been made and Castaldi again contacted Mahanna and without naming Saunders told him he had lined up a local printer who agreed to run off the stamps. The only thing needed to get the printing going was an advance payment to purchase supplies and some necessary equipment.

Secret Service agents advised the inspectors that all the persons involved in this case, with the possible exception of Saunders, were suspected of having organized crime connections. This was further supported by developments in New York. After Mahanna had agreed to cooperate with the inspectors and Secret Service agents, the attorney who showed up at an arraignment was an identified Mob lawyer.

It was believed that Mahanna had not arranged for this attorney to be present. Apparently, other individuals felt they needed their interests to be protected. The attorney bargained for dismissal of the charges in exchange for Mahanna's cooperation. An agreement was finally made whereby Mahanna would not be required to testify in any court proceeding. In return, Mahanna would cooperate in future counterfeit investigations. I would not hold my breath for that to occur.

This is one of the frustrating things about not having access to Secret Service files. The explanation given for what happened in New York makes little sense at all. Just maybe, however, it could be the explanation of what happened to the New York counterfeiting operation. All through the 1970s in that suspect location, one stamp after another was coming off of what is believed to be a mystery press. Then all activity appeared to suddenly stop. This is another unresolved mystery the answer to which is most likely buried somewhere in the files of the Secret Service.

This was a victory for the New York Secret Service and U.S. Attorney's office. They may have been very satisfied with Mahanna's agreement, but it is questionable if St. Louis would have been as thrilled when informed. The immediate fear would be that the "Mob's" attorney would have learned the details of the investigation. If Mahanna failed to fully cooperate, or if someone in New York decided to inform St. Louis of the New York arrests, the St. Louis investigation could be dead in the water. Fortunately it appears this did not happen.

The St. Louis investigation did continue. Over the weekend on July 31 to August 1, 1982, telephone arrangements were made between Mahanna and Castaldi for an advance payment to be made to Castaldi in St. Louis. He agreed to print the stamps and make delivery the following weekend, but he insisted on having $5,000 up front money. When the agreed-upon payment did not arrive as scheduled, another delay occurred. This resulted in numerous phone calls going back and forth. Finally, via Express mail the money got there and everything was back on schedule.

While all the above was going on, surveillance of the Saunders Printing Shop had kicked into high gear. When it was concluded this facility would be the key to operations; agents had been pulled back from following Castaldi, Saputo (a third individual identified), and Fink so their surveillance would not be blown. Agents concluded that due to the number of employees and the amount of foot traffic that went in and out of the building, it was surmised the printing would most likely occur either early in the morning or after 8 p.m.

On August 5, Castaldi called Mahanna and verified that the money had arrived. He told Mahanna that he had given the money to Saputo and it would be used to purchase materials for the counterfeit operation. He further relayed they had already completed some of the printing, and more would be finished that evening. The agents agreed this was the green light and they would hit the printing plant that evening.

On a number of occasions Saputo had been observed visiting the print shop and meeting with Saunders. Then on the evening of August 5, Saputo was observed arriving in the vicinity, and then going into a nearby restaurant. About an hour later, Saunders also arrived, spent some time inside the print shop, and then joined Saputo in the restaurant. At about 9 p.m., both men returned to the print shop. The agents gave them about 20 minutes, and then they made their own entry. Task Force agents immediately placed both men under arrest.

Saunders really was not a criminal at heart. With very little encouragement from the agents, he rolled over and admitted his participation in the counterfeit operation, naming Saputo and another person later identified as Vincent S. Scognamiglio as participants in the operation. He also gave the agents a consent to search the facility.

The agents took their time in their search, and it was worthwhile. They found six negatives, three counterfeit printing plates, $3,265.00 in finished stamps, the printing press, and at least 1,000 blank sheets of gummed paper ready to be used. Later that evening Saunders would surrender his invoices that showed he had purchased 18,000 sheets of gummed paper that he acknowledged had already been used in printing additional counterfeit stamps.

Saunders provided a statement to the agents in which he described his total involvement in this enterprise. As he told his story he initially had been approached by Saputo in December of 1981. Saputo had represented to him that they simply were going to produce some Easter Seal type stamps that would be used for charity purposes. They discussed what equipment would be needed and if there would be any problems in making items of this nature. It was only after all the arrangements had been made for the delivery of equipment that Saunders suddenly realized their true target was going to be postage stamps. By then he felt he was in too deeply to back out and he agreed to go along with this criminal enterprise.

Knowing his best chance for leniency was to cooperate fully, Saunders went on to describe how he photographed stamps for the preparation of negatives and plates. Then, at Saputo's direction, he had printed various denominations of stamps. Once the printing was done, the stamps were turned over to Saputo. Where they had gone from there he did not know, but earlier in the day Saputo had informed him he had a new outlet for additional stamps. Most likely this was the New York order.

A new day had dawned in organized crime. Just about everyone involved in this saga had no problem rolling over on their partners in crime. Saputo took investigators to his home where he surrendered $2,800 worth of counterfeit stamps. He then made oral admissions naming Castaldi, Fink, and Scognamiglio as other participants in the counterfeit operation. Castaldi and Fink would be arrested later on August 5, 1982, but Scognamiglio could not immediately be found. The very next day Saputo, Saunders, Castaldi and Fink appeared in

U.S. District Court for a bond setting. Saunders and Saputo were released on $5,000 recognizance bonds; Fink was released on a $50,000 surety bond; and Castaldi was held in lieu of a $50,000 cash or surety bond. Scognamiglio was finally picked up on August 10 and the same day he was released on a $50,000 bond.

Negatives for the printing of counterfeit stamps were seized in 5-cent, 17-cent, 18-cent, 20-cent, and 37-cent denominations. An interesting question presented was how much it had cost to set up this counterfeiting operation. Apparently to get a new printing operation off the ground it was not all that much. The Rosback round hole perforator was obtained for $100. The A.B. Dick offset press Model 360CD cost $1,700. The NuArc Platemaker was $350. Other odds and ends were already on hand as they would be in any printing shop.

Once again, when the government's agents figured out what was going on, it was like tugging on a loose string. Everything began to unravel. Everyone threw everyone else under the bus. What had been a very successful operation possibly for years was brought to a screeching close. How much damage was done before this adventure was finally concluded is another question. Most likely we are talking about millions in lost revenue to the U.S Postal Service. As stories go, one could only wish all the others would be as entertaining as this one was.

A point that needs to be hammered home is that this little St. Louis enterprise had been going on for a number of years. Most likely this operation had cost the Postal Service millions in lost revenue all by itself. For those in the stamp world who have scoffed at the quality and quantity of counterfeit stamps, the results speak for themselves. Tell me how many of the following have been found?

These are the stamps that are known to have been counterfeited just in this one venture:

5-cent Washington

17-cent Carson

18-cent Mason

20-cent "C" Eagle

20-cent Bunche

37-cent Millikan

Looking at the case summaries, the impression I was left with was this could be just the tip of the iceberg. Many more stamp varieties have been duplicated over the years of operation without detection.

Any takers?

The Secret Service vs. the Post Office

For more than a hundred years the Secret Service had things pretty much their own way. They investigated counterfeiting and nobody really thought that much about it. With the Post Office there was little if any conflict. The Secret Service started out as a very small and overworked organization, and as such, their agents worked very well with the postal inspectors, and most others for that matter. It was after the Kennedy assassination that things would begin to change. The Secret Service would grow from a few hundred agents scattered across the country, but primarily in Washington, to some 3,500 agents today, with a separate uniform division primarily located in D.C.

When I entered federal law enforcement, the Secret Service was still recovering from the event in Dallas. Our agencies worked very closely with one another. Frequently, inspectors would be drafted as support in protective duties. Both of our agencies investigated theft and forgery of Treasury Checks and other federal obligation because they frequently were stolen from the mail.

As a new inspector I had a good working relationship with an agent in West Texas. We jointly investigated cases and even alternated writing the prosecution documents for those cases we were taking to Federal Court. This system worked well for our mutual benefit. It was only when our agencies began to step on each other's toes in counterfeit postage investigations that conflict would arise between the Secret Service and the postal inspectors.

The Secret Service was originally created to investigate the counterfeiting of our currency, and stamps were simply an afterthought. Where currency is concerned they are very effective. An advantage you have with money is that the counterfeit currency in this country will eventually always be identified either in banks or the Federal Reserve. Once a bill is identified, they can chase the individuals passing them on the street, and work their way back to the presses. Unfortunately, this frequently does not happen with stamps.

Stamps historically have been classified as an obligation of the government, and the Secret Service frequently treated stamp cases exactly the same as a currency investigation. The problem is, they are not the same. You might arrest people selling or distributing bogus stamps on the street. You may even work your way back to a press; still, the problem has not been resolved. Counterfeit stamps will still be out there, and used in the mail, and the odds are they will not be detected. Very simply, nobody looks at a stamp. Over and again, agents and Treasury officials have made the comment, "Why would someone copy a stamp?" This attitude simply reflects the degree of importance given by the Secret Service to most any stamp investigation.

For both postal management and that of the Inspection Service, the thinking was much the same. First, counterfeit postage was not viewed as a problem. After all, who would bother to copy a stamp? Then more importantly, why should we expend either our manpower or resources to deal with stamp counterfeiting when we have this other very capable organization, the Secret Service, which is more than willing to carry our water? If postal management thought about counterfeiting at all, which I concluded they did not, the philosophy of both management and the Inspection Service was simply summed up:

If you do not look for counterfeits, you will not find them.

If you do not find them, they do not exist.

If they do not exist, you do not need to look for them.

On my own part, I fell into counterfeit stamp investigations. Not only was I fascinated by this crime, I was also an unusual commodity within the Inspection Service. I was a stamp collector. Then I did the unthinkable. I turned over the rock and started to swat at all the scorpions that scurried out. When I started, all I was trying to do was find out what had happened in the past so I would be able to answer questions in court. Then when I began to look at the record, it soon seemed to me that this was a crime that had patterns. A reasonable conclusion was that if these patterns could be identified it just might give us a leg up on future investigation. After all, why should every inspector suddenly confronted with a new counterfeit case have to reinvent the wheel? Unfortunately, that is exactly what inspectors had been forced to do in case after case.

Cases had ranged from just a few dollars to multimillion dollar operations. Many of these were criminal operations that may have gone on for years without detection. It was not simply the size of these cases, but the sheer number that totally blew my mind. Ultimately, it would be evident that just about every regular issue stamp had at one time or another been duplicated. Many of these items had been copied multiple times by different individuals.

What had been occurring with stamp counterfeiting is the perfect crime. Nobody either in officialdom or the general public even comprehended that this activity was going on. It was easy to understand how infrequently this activity would be discovered. Just ask yourself how critically do we look at a common stamp? Back before the days of postal mechanization, the average piece of mail would be physically handled about 19 times before delivery. In the 1950s mechanization of postal operations began, and now a mailed article can literally go through the system without ever being touched by human hands. Very simply nobody in the Post Office has the assignment to actually look at and judge the validity of a stamp. The opportunity for the perfect crime has been created.

When the authorities have discovered a postal counterfeit, not uncommonly they were investigating some other offense. When it was a case the Secret Service was working on, not surprisingly this was a currency case. That is what they are concerned with. Inevitably, when bogus currency is found, the postage stamps, if not outright ignored, generally are pushed aside or the significance minimized when it is time for prosecution. If noted at all by the media, if you are lucky, you may find one or two sentences worth of ink mentioning their existence.

Even in the Inspection Service, counterfeit stamps would generally be considered an orphan child. None of the investigative units, like fraud, external, internal theft, or audit would consistently claim responsibility for this criminal offense. When counterfeit stamp activity was discovered, the general consensus was to let the Secret Service worry about it. Some inspector frequently picked at random would be given the task to follow along and file a case report. The problem this presented was when I began to research and then write about these cases, this would upset the apple cart.

The Secret Service may have done a more than adequate job protecting the currency of the country. Unfortunately, the approach used for currency does not work all that well with stamps. Counterfeit stamps could float through the mail stream for years, long after a particular case may have been declared over and done. Besides, time and again the same individuals would return to this particular endeavor, and nobody really kept track of them.

In an attempt to bring counterfeiting activity and other revenue problems to the attention of management, year after year, I and other inspectors would submit reports outlining the extent of the problem. The feeling was that these reports commonly would die somewhere in the bureaucracy of Washington. As a field inspector in Chicago, I continued to do my own thing, investigating cases and periodically checking the mail to see what could be found. As I researched both old and new cases I did the unpardonable crime. I began to publish these stories in both the general and in various philatelic publications. At some point an article apparently found its way to the attention of the Postmaster General. The story that came back to me was one day the PMG pointedly asked the Chief Inspector, "What's this about our having a counterfeit postage problem?"

In the late 1970s, the Inspection Service management was dragged kicking and screaming to the recognition that there was a revenue protection problem. At least that was the impression I came away with. When they seriously started to look, inspectors all over the country were finding counterfeit cases. As we tried to take a more proactive role in the resolution of those problems the Secret Service pushed back. That is not a reflection of the Secret Service doing anything wrong. In their view, they simply were protecting turf that historically they viewed as their own. Now suddenly, the inspectors were butting into the mix, and some agents resisted this effort. Originally postal bureaucrats supported Treasury bureaucrats, but eventually a breaking point was reached. This is exemplified by a report submitted by an inspector in Miami. Again, many of the names have been removed for obvious reasons.

1. This report is in response to a telephone call received on – from AIC – that I should explain why I did not notify the U.S. Secret Service of my intentions to locate and question – in the state of Massachusetts, relative to a joint counterfeit investigation. AIC – directed that I should also explain why I did not conduct the Massachusetts part of the investigation jointly with the U.S. Secret Service.

2. The reasons are complex and the answers cannot be stated in a few words. All of the counterfeit stamps that were detected and recovered in this case were in the mail stream or had been in the mail stream and returned to the sender. The discovery of the counterfeit stamps was made by the Postal Service and the U.S. Secret Service was invited to join in the investigation. Since the return card bore the name of the Fraternal Order of Police, detectives of the Dade County Public Safety Department, Organized Crime Bureau, were invited to participate in this investigation by me. Their contribution to the overall investigation effort has been far better than that of the Secret Service.

3. Assistant Special Agent in Charge – of the U.S. Secret Service at Miami, Florida, assigned S/A – to work with me in this case. From the very beginning, he was authoritative and he made it clear that this was his case and he intended to call the shots. It was obvious to me that he had little concern for the other agencies involved or their particular interest or problems in the case, such as the possible mail fraud aspect of the case or the concern the Public Safety Department detectives had, that this was a sensitive matter for them in that the Fraternal Order of Police name was being used in these mailings.

4. The problems experienced with the U.S. Secret Service in this case were explained in detail in a preliminary report on April 7, 1978, and a copy of that report is attached herewith. I believe that this problem is far more than a personality clash between S/A – and myself.

5. Practically all Secret Service agents are convinced that their agency has exclusive jurisdiction in any counterfeit case and they make their position very clear. Since our regulations say that inspectors share joint jurisdiction with the U.S. Secret Service in counterfeit stamp cases, there is obviously a conflict between the two agencies at a national level, which causes a bad problem in the field. Not only does this case point that out, but I have talked to several inspectors in other Divisions and in other Regions who have experienced similar problems. Recently a Secret Service agent testified

from the stand in the Federal District Court at Chicago that the U.S. Secret Service has exclusive jurisdiction in counterfeit cases ...

6. Under the circumstances, as they were in the case assigned to me, I felt duty-bound to protect the postal service interest and in the case of counterfeit stamps in general, the postal service is the ultimate victim when the stamps have been used. To demonstrate that the attitude of the U.S. Secret Service in counterfeit stamp cases goes beyond that of just one isolated agent (S/A –), I have read the report of S/A Fred B. Simpson of Columbia, South Carolina, dated April 10, 1978, in which he made the following statement: "I then explained to (inspector) Williams that the Postal Inspection Service does not investigate counterfeit United States postage stamps.

7. On the very first evening when I met S/A –, we conducted a surveillance and after conducting that surveillance, a discussion was had about the obtaining of a search warrant and the timing and the serving of the search warrant. We were discussing the aspects of probable cause when S/A – remarked that he could not detect a counterfeit stamp if he saw one. S/A – stated that he wanted to serve the search warrant as soon as possible and I injected several ideas as to why I thought we should briefly delay the serving of the search warrant from Friday until Monday. It was at this time that S/A – stated the following: "Let's look at it this way, unless we come up with 100,000 stamps, what's in it for me?" In these statements he left me with several distinct impressions, as follows:

(a) That he knew very little about counterfeit stamp investigations.

(b) That he was going to take charge regardless.

(c) That he was in a hurry to get the investigation over with so that he could get on to bigger and better things.

(d) That he had little or no concern about problems or concerns of the other agencies involved.

8. On March 3, 1978, a search warrant was served in this case. S/A – took control of all evidence/exhibits obtained in the search. He did not furnish me any copies of the affidavit that he took from the manager of the local operation where the search warrant was served, Mr. ... in turn, I took a statement from the young lady who was the secretary of the operation where the search was made and I did not furnish him a copy.

9. The circumstances that stopped all communications between S/A – and me occurred on March 10, which are as follows: A telephone call was received by Senior Stenographer Joyce Baker at the Miami Domicile for S/A –, who requested to talk to me. At that moment, we were having a brief ceremony for one of our postal inspectors who was leaving the service and Ms. Baker asked S/A – if it would be all right for me to return his call in a few minutes. S/A – became very sarcastic and demanding, stating that he was calling on official business and that he was not hanging up. He remarked sarcastically that it must be great when an agency can take time out during the day to have a party. When I got to the phone, he wanted to know the name of the young lady that I had taken the sworn statement from on the night of the serving of the search warrant. He was also curt and sarcastic to me and he obviously was sitting at his desk dictating a report and needed the name of this person to complete his report.

RECENT DEVELOPMENTS

10. On June 7, 1978, a telecopier message was received from the INC Atlanta Division, which was a copy of a directive received from the Chief Inspector, USPS, Washington, D.C. That directive states among other things that any further presentations to a United States Attorney's office in this case would be made jointly with the U.S. Secret Service. In response to that directive, AIC D.C. Jones met with Special Agent in Charge Charles Howell, U.S. Secret Service, on June 9, 1978, at which time copies of all affidavits, memorandums of interview, 15 counterfeit stamps, and copies of other tangible evidence, were furnished to the U.S. Secret Service. At that time the U.S. Secret Service furnished at my request, a copy of the affidavit of –

11. In response to my request to keep this case moving, I met with SAIC Charles Howell, AIC Arthur Rivers, and S/A – on June 20, 1978. At that time, I asked them for copies of all other statements and memorandums of interview that they had obtained and they furnished same to me. This meeting came about because I had called SAIC Howell and S/A –, stating that I thought we should get together and prepare a list of witnesses and a list of exhibits preparatory to presenting this matter to the U.S. Attorney's office. When I first got to the Secret Service office, I was taken to AIC River's office, who stated that he had instructions from his Headquarters in the Counterfeit Section, Washington, that the U.S. Secret Service would

present this matter to the U.S. Attorney without the Inspection Service and that the Inspection Service would in no way be allowed to participate in the presentation of this matter to the U.S. Attorney's office, since the U.S. Secret Service has exclusive jurisdiction of Title 18, Section, 501, U.S. Code. I told Mr. Rivers that this was contrary to the directive from the Chief Inspector, and that I could not abide by such an agreement. I came back to the office and reported this matter by telephone to INC W.F. Hanson. He later called me and stated that he had been in touch with SAIC Howell, who called his office in Washington and that the Secret Service had now agreed that the matter be presented jointly to the U.S. Attorney's Office.

12. While at the Secret Service Office on June 20, 1978, S/A – and myself shook hands and agreed that everything that had transpired was past history and that we would start our relationship anew and work together on this case in the future. (Yes, and lions will lie down with lambs.)

SUMMARY

13. Based on the facts as stated herein, I did not communicate or coordinate any part of the investigation with the U.S. Secret Service after March 10, 1978, for the reasons as follows:

(a) To protect the interest of the Postal Service.

(b) To stand up for the dignity and reputation of postal inspectors.

(c) To stand up for the dignity and respect of one of our staff people who was abused by S/A –.

(d) The relationship was not a two-way street. It was one in which the U.S. Secret Service took all and gave nothing. They had not furnished me copies of anything that came out of the search or the affidavit obtained from –.

(e) The success of this investigation was being hampered by S/A – who wanted to get the investigation over with so he could move on to bigger and better things. Had it not been for the outstanding investigative efforts of inspector Bill Williams, Columbia, South Carolina, the U.S. Secret Service would have closed their case with no potential prosecution and they would have been satisfied to do so. All they had obtained out of their Columbia office was a negative affidavit (worthless) and it was inspector Williams' follow up investigation that got this case moving.

The inspector waging this valiant battle with the Secret Service in Miami was R.S. Weaver. The mistake the Secret Service made was going to battle with a very capable and senior agent who knew his stuff and would not back down. The lesson to really take from this event is that if the Post Office is depending on the Secret Service to protect their revenue they have a real problem. This is the norm. They simply are not interested in stamps. Oh, another comment here. Miami was the key that unlocked what was occurring in the Northeast, the Boston press, and the stamps he was dealing with were the 13-cent Kennedy and the Liberty Bell.

The Secret Service is not being attacked here. That organization was in the midst of rapid expansion and was facing a multitude of challenges. Understandably, both long-term agents and the new recruits were very defensive of their investigative responsibilities. This had put the Secret Service and the Inspection Service on a collision course. It was becoming evident that protecting postal revenue and following these cases to their conclusion was not a high priority for the Secret Service and the Inspection Service needed to look after its own revenue.

The Secret Service really had its hands full. Besides the run-of-the mill home grown counterfeits, some new challenges were rapidly developing. For years the Treasury Department had stymied the development and commercialization of colored copiers. When they finally hit the public market there was, and would continue to be, an explosion of street-corner counterfeiting. Now virtually every Tom, Dick, and Harry, for the expenditure of a few hundred dollars, could overnight make his own money (and stamps). Added to what was going on inside the country, the real challenge to our nation's financial integrity was coming from other countries. Hundreds of millions of virtually undetectable dollars were being manufactured in Latin America, Eastern Europe, and the Middle East. Later it would be found that North Korea and possibly China had entered the mix. These challenges are ongoing.

Finally both postal management and the Inspection Service

recognized they had a problem that needed to be addressed. The Chief Inspector made a valiant effort to hammer out ground rules with the Secret Service. Needless to say this met with resistance. Finally the Chief Inspector simply issued his own directive to inspectors in the field:

AGREEMENT BETWEEN THE UNITED STATES SECRET SERVICE AND THE UNITED STATES POSTAL INSPECTION SERVICE PERTAINING TO INVESTIGATIONS OF CASES INVOLVING COUNTERFEIT POSTAGE STAMPS

1. Jurisdiction

   A. Pursuant to the provisions of section 3056, title 18, United States Code, the Secret Service is authorized to detect and arrest any person committing any offense against the laws of the United States relating to obligations and securities of the United States and/or foreign governments.

   B. Pursuant to the provision of section 404, title 39, section 3061, title 18, United States Code, Postal Inspectors are authorized to investigate postal offenses and make arrests for postal offenses.

2. Purpose of Agreement

   The Postal Inspection Service and the U.S. Secret Service have cooperated in joint investigations of postage stamp counterfeiting and rendered valuable support to the other in carrying out their investigative responsibilities. The purpose of the agreement is to provide procedures and guidelines for joint investigations, cooperative assistance and mutual exchange of information between the Secret Service and Postal Inspection Service relative to the counterfeiting of U.S. postage stamps.

3. Exchange of Information

   Both agencies shall immediately advise the other of any information they may receive relative to the counterfeiting of postage stamps.

4. Investigative assistance

Both agencies will participate in joint investigations of counterfeiting of postage stamps extending full investigative cooperation including continuing exchange of information. Whenever either agency is unable to participate in the investigation for any reason, the other agency shall proceed with the investigation being cognizant of collateral issued or other violations affecting the absent agency and proceeding in a manner that will not jeopardize or adversely affect the absent agency's interest or responsibilities.

5. Implementing Instructions

   The United States Secret Service and the United States Postal Inspectors shall issue appropriate instructions for the guidance of their personnel in implementing the provisions of this agreement.

The Secret Service may not have liked it, but they were given notice this was the way business would be conducted in the future. Finally the Inspection Service was stating these cases would be investigated by the Inspection Service, and if the Secret Service did not like this, that was unfortunate.

6

The Contraband Postage Identification Program

The Postal Reorganization Act of 1970 abolished the United States Post Office Department, a part of the cabinet, and created the United States Postal Service, a corporation – like an independent agency with an official monopoly on the delivery of mail in the United States. The first paragraph of the act reads:

> The United States Postal Service shall be operated as a basic and fundamental service provided to the people by the Government of the United States, authorized by the Constitution, created by an Act of Congress, and supported by the people. The Postal Service shall have as its basic function the obligation to provide postal services to bind the Nation together through the personal, educational, literary, and business correspondence of the people. It shall provide prompt, reliable, and efficient service to patrons in all areas and shall render postal service to all communities. The cost of establishing and maintaining the Postal Service shall not be apportioned to impair the overall value of such service to the people.

The Postal Service was now expected to pay its own way. The organization no longer had a blank check with the nation's treasury. The revenue of the Postal Service is primarily derived from the sale and use of postal products. In the 1970s, when case after case of counterfeit postage was discovered, it became clear concerted action was required to address this problem.

In the spring of 1983, the Criminal Investigation Division at Headquarters began studying the effectiveness of the Inspection Service in revenue protection efforts. There was a growing concern about the number and complexity of the cases being found. This included counterfeiting of postage, reuse of postage, and fencing of legitimate postage stock taken in robberies and burglaries. There was even a security problem discovered in the stamp-destruction process. Added to the aforementioned was the increasing awareness that there was insufficient accountability being given to postage meters. A tipping point had finally been reached where these problems could no longer be swept under the rug.

Digging into old cases presented a glimpse at some of the warning shots fired across the bow of the old Post Office Department, and its offspring – the United States Postal Service.

Minneapolis 1962

A Classic Story in Free Enterprise

Back in audit training, minimal attention was given to meter verifications. Surprisingly, something that was never addressed was the subject of manipulation or even counterfeits. Looking back it is easy to see why. Postage meters have long been perceived as a secure way to dispense postage to businesses by the Post Office. You could not buy a meter; it had to be leased from one of the licensed suppliers. When you as a meter holder need postage, you must bring your machine into your local post office that maintains the records for that machine. The important point is that you buy the postage you use up front, and use it as needed. It is a program that on its face appeared to be tightly controlled.

On October 16, 1963, one hole in the system was exposed. Postal Inspector Gosnell had made a routine stop at Addressing and Mailing, a large mail preparation business in Minneapolis, Minnesota. As a normal part of any financial audit an inspector for meter verification is required to look at a sample of meters assigned to the post office being audited. This was just a routine stop to pick up a sample of their meter impressions to put into his audit file. On his way out the door he was stopped by an employee who asked a simple question: "Is it really okay if we print a copy of the meter stamp, and then apply it to a mailing we are preparing?" Not sure how Gosnell responded, but I do know that shortly thereafter, a number of inspectors would descend on this facility.

Addressing and Mailing was a direct mail preparation service that handled the mass mailing needs of many large-volume mailers in the Twin Cities area. These were businesses and public institutions that frequently were putting out tens of thousands of mailing pieces on a regular basis. The owner and operator was identified as Francis O. Olson, who frequently hired as his employees several young men whom he paid a basic minimum wage.[46]

The business was structured into two parts. In one section of the building there was a printing plant where they would create many of the mailing pieces for their customers. These were things like return addresses, letterheads, advertising material, and the general inserts for their customers. In the other part of the business they did the actual mail preparation. At the trial several of Olson's employees would testify they were instructed by Olson to print something else. It was the postage meter impressions that would appear on the envelopes. These impressions were coming off of a printing press, not a meter machine.

It appears that at some point Olson had concluded that he could cut his mailing costs and easily circumvent the security of the Post Office. After all, right at hand he had readily available all the equipment he needed. This was the same brainstorm that Anton Winter had way back in the 1930s, or for that matter possibly even Warren Thomson back in 1894. Looking at his printing press, Olson concluded he could easily print his own postage. What is more, a meter impression is so much easier to duplicate than a stamp.[47] When he instructed his employees to do this, many of them questioned if this was really legal. His response was, "Don't worry." He said he would pay the Post Office for his mailings after he was paid by his customers.

Olson's process was very simple. First, you simply run an envelope through your meter machine to get a good clean impression. Then, take a picture of the envelope, particularly the image of the meter. With offset printing, that negative is then laid against a metal plate and the image is transferred. This is how your printing plate is created. On the offset press, as this metal plate with the impression on it goes around, ink is picked up on the image. The cylinder with the plate would then transfer the image onto a rubber mat on another cylinder. When that rubber mat came against the envelope, the image of the postage meter was transferred to the envelope. This was a basic

46 A point to be remembered here: If you are going to be involved in criminal activity, it might be a good idea if you at least pay your employees a living wage.

47 Someone really should tell the Postal Service Retail Division about this. Have you recently looked at some of the items being authorized as postage? Yes, Congress, the Post Office still has a problem.

description of how offset printing works, and it would be presented to the jury in the Olson case.

Again, this was not a small operation. We are talking about millions of pieces of mail for which no payment had been made. The investigation found that on a regular basis Olson would direct his employees to photograph the meter impression, make a new plate, and run the envelopes for a specific mailing they had been contracted to put out. Reportedly after each mailing had been done, Olson would put the plate and negative in a file he maintained in his office. After Inspector Gosnell's original visit, Olson must have suspected he had been discovered. When the inspectors returned to Address and Mailing this file had disappeared.

Reviewing the trial transcript one discovers that the U.S. Attorney presents a good training guide on how meter machines function, and how meter records were maintained. This was one of the first things the prosecutors had to get across to the jury. At the facility, Gosnell seized the ledger books for the two Pitney Bowes meter machines leased to Address and Mailing. The reading on the meters would be compared to what was in both the Post Office records for settings and the book assigned to each machine.

The jury heard how the machines functioned and how the various sequence counters on the machines worked. Every time a piece of mail went through the machine the dial turned over once and this would be documented in the sequence counter. Then there were two other dials on the machine that registered the dollars and cents. One was called the descending register, and the other the ascending register. When a meter is brought into the Post Office the postal clerk will increase the descending register to reflect the amount of postage you have purchased. As the postage is used this register goes down until it reaches zero, and the machine will automatically lock out until more postage is purchased. Your ascending register reflects the total amount of postage that has ever been run through a given machine. Olson circumvented the entire process by basically not using the machine, except to make his initial meter strip that would be duplicated.

A real simple check for inspectors would be to compare the amount of postage purchased in the records to the registers on the machines. The only problem there is that when audits are conducted you just check a sample of customer meters. In a large office like Minneapolis, there could be thousands of meters assigned to it. Another verification would be to compare the amount of mail prepared and dropped off for delivery with the amount of postage purchased by a specific company. Good luck with that. Unless you have a specific suspicion this never would happen.

When it came to charging Olson the government presented 10 counts that related to the reproduction of postage meter impressions (counterfeiting). Then, in a second indictment another crime was alleged. "The government is going to prove that these first 10 incidents were also (some of them) part of a bigger scheme because not only didn't the government get paid for the postage printed on those envelopes, but the customers in many cases paid for postage that was never used and by false representations billed for by the Addressing and Mailing Company." This is mail fraud.

In proving the case against Olson probably the most devastating testimony was given by his employees. They would relate not only how the counterfeit impressions had been made but also provided damaging comments on the number of incidents and the size of the mailings. This testimony complimented that of the inspectors that described the postal records and how large the revenue losses to the Post Office was suspected of being. The issue never really was in doubt and Olson was convicted. He would be sentenced to five years in the custody of the Attorney General.

Years later a common refrain I heard is how can one identify a counterfeit meter impression? If it is a single piece, and in the mail, it is very, very hard. If you catch the counterfeits before they get into the mails, your chances are much better. The first thing to look for is the quality of the impression. Jokingly I have commented, "If it is clean and precise there is a good chance it is bogus." If you have multiple envelopes another question is, Is the meter impression in exactly the same position on your mailing pieces? If so, you may have photo duplication that came off a printing press. With a legitimate meter the impression will move both up and down, and side to side, as each individual envelope goes through a meter machine.

Boston – New York, 1966

Meter Manipulation

If either the U.S. Postal Service or the U.S. Postal Inspection Service really took meter security seriously, one would think the training of inspectors would cover this area more extensively. To be honest, little if any attention to this important area was covered in our training. It was really learned on the job, and I left training with no real understanding of the problem. The extent of what we learned in the classroom was mostly limited to understanding how the registers work, how postage is put on the machine, and how to verify the meter totals in the postal accounts. Little attention, if any, was given to security of the machines themselves. It would become obvious that nobody in Washington was thinking about meter security either. In training, no mention at all was made to how these machines could be manipulated.

If photographic duplication or the utilization of an offset press was not enough, a case I would later find involved how to manipulate a mechanical meter. Someone had finally built a better mouse trap. A little snippet in the New York Times led me to a court file. On March 9, 1966, a Grand Jury indictment came down that charged:

> Bernard Abelson, Leonard Lewis and Ira and Lila Ravner with unlawfully, willfully and knowingly, combine, conspire, confederate and agree together with each other and with diverse other persons unknown to the Grand Jury to defraud the United States Post Office Department, to commit offenses against the United States, to violate Title 18, United States Code, Section 501.
>
> It was a part of said conspiracy that the defendants unlawfully, willfully and knowingly would defraud the United States and the United States Post Office Department of money by means of printing and using as postage in the mailing of mail matter Pitney Bowes postage meter stamp impressions which were counterfeited, which were not authorized by the Post Office Department and for which no payment was made nor would be made.

An important point of law here. When you put something on an envelope that purports to be valid payment of postage, and you have not made the appropriate payment to the Post Office, that is counterfeiting.

It appears that this criminal operation began in 1962, in Watertown, Massachusetts when defendant Abelson and Lila Ravner tampered with a Pitney Bowes meter machine. They continued to operate this illegal enterprise in Massachusetts until sometime in 1964, when Lila married the defendant, Ira Ravner. They then transferred their operation to New York City. Postal inspectors would conservatively estimate that the Post Office had been defrauded in the amount of $2 million during the operation of the scheme in New York and Boston.

These were not hardened professional criminals. This was simply a very intelligent businessman who operated a mail-order clothing business, first in Boston and then in New York. Like many before and after, he realized that his business would be so much more profitable if he did not need to pay for his mailing costs. He was using a Pitney Bowes mechanical postage meter. One day when he played with the device he discovered how the mechanical machine could be manipulated to give postage without being reflected in the registers.

Having been arrested and now going to trial, the defendants were forced to look at reality. Before they could be found guilty, these three defendants changed their pleas to guilty. Not surprisingly, in return they requested their sentences be reduced. Even with these pleas, Bernard N. Abelson had been sentenced to three years and fined $22,000. Ira Ravner received six months and a fine of $12,000. Lila Ravner received a sentence of one year and a day, plus a fine of $22,000. The government would agree to a sentence reduction only if they offered material assistance in making cases against other individuals in Boston who were former associates.

The government would get more than codefendant testimony here. By pleading guilty it was reasoned the inspectors could suppress the details on how these machines could be compromised. This was something the defendants could hold over the head of the government. It was argued that if this happened, very possibly this would destroy the usefulness of the meter machines as a dispenser of postage.

In Boston two additional defendants would be indicted. The charge was at the Boston end of things where operations began on or about March 1, 1963. Again, the susceptibility of the meter machine to manipulation was not addressed. At both the Post Office Department and Pitney Bowes someone had decided everyone could pretend nothing significant had occurred here. Business would go on as usual and no corrective answers or accountability was demanded. The Post Office kept secret how these machines could be manipulated, even from their own inspectors. Twenty years later it would be discovered that others would make the same discovery.

An interesting note was that Abelson and his primary codefendant partner in Boston were not folks one would generally identify as candidates for being common street criminals. Both these men were intelligent young men who were graduates of Harvard. Most likely they did not even consider what they were doing as criminal. All they wanted to do was cut their postage costs. In today's world they would have felt right at home on Wall Street.

At the conclusion of the case, United States Attorney Robert M. Morgenthau had made an interesting observation: "Everyone thought these machines were foolproof." What would not become public knowledge was that virtually every mechanical meter could be manipulated. Just in this case, in New York, the inspectors did just a ball park estimate of revenue loss based on the amount of mail they had seized and the identified period of operation. This was computed to be $1 million, conservatively.

As time went by things did not improve for Abelson. Looking at court files it was discovered in 1972 that Abelson again had legal problems. This time it was with the IRS. It seems that when he filed his income taxes, to support his claim for a refund he had submitted a number of cancelled checks. The only problem presented was that when the IRS looked at these documents, they discovered that the amounts had been altered. Once again this is called fraud, and this time the IRS would call it tax evasion.

Arthur Franken, Los Angeles 1972

A Simple Idea Returns

Then a man came along who proved you really do not even need a machine. In 1972, Arthur Franken was arrested and charged with counterfeiting meter impressions. This was a scheme that Franken had been utilizing for a number of years in the conduct of his mail order sex toy business. Soon after he started to sell these items through mail order, Franken got upset with the cost of his postage and began to explore other ideas. He first experimented with rubber stamp impressions that were reasonably successful. Still, not satisfied, he eventually migrated to using engraved metal plates. In either case, using either a rubber stamp or metal plates, Franken discovered how easy it was to create his own meter impression.

To create a metal meter plate Franken utilized the same idea first pioneered by E. Louis Smith with his counterfeit postal cards back in 1902. Both Franken and Smith had placed orders with various companies that would make metal engravings. Both these individuals had then done a cut and paste to create their own meter impression. Smith had created actual counterfeit printing plates for his printing press. Franken simply mounted his metal plate on a wooden block that he could roll across the envelopes or parcels he was sending out.

Eventually one of the companies making Franken's metal plate impressions put two and two together and figured something bogus was going on. They notified the inspectors. When the inspectors moved in they would estimate that the revenue loss to the Post Office for his period of operation, January 1966 to November 1972, amounted to at least $720,000. Not bad for a work-at-home scheme.

When I last heard of Franken, he had relocated to Mexico and was then running another get-rich-quick scam down there. I do not remember exactly what idea he came up with next, but selling ice cubes to Eskimos came to my mind. I think it had something to do with home heating units. The last I heard he still owed restitution to the Post Office.

Anaheim, California 1983

Back to Stamps, and Porn, and Currency

One night mail handler, Thomas Shugart, noted that approximately 1,200 pieces of mail were not being canceled by the Mark II facer canceling machine. When he examined the envelopes, he observed that they all appeared to originate from one mailer. Shugart thought this was suspicious, so he brought his concern to the attention of John Hill, the Supervisor of Mails at the facility. The supervisor agreed that something was strange here. He pulled the items out of the mail and promptly contacted the local postal inspectors. The return address on the suspected envelopes was the R.B. Company, 2170 W. Broadway in Anaheim, California.

On March 14, 1983, the mail being held by the Post Office was inspected by Postal Inspector James G. Earnest. Using a black light, Inspector Earnest and Postal Supervisor W. Thornton checked the mail. They determined that the 20-cent flag stamps affixed as postage had no phosphor tagging. When they examined the stamps under a magnifying glass, they soon concluded these items appeared different from similar stamps they pulled out of the postal accountability.

It was at this point that Mr. Thornton informed the inspector that he knew of two previous mailings, one on February 7, and another on February 9, believed to have originated from the same company. He remembered that those stamps were not being properly cancelled either. They had to be run through a manual canceling machine. Those mailings had totaled approximately 3,000 and 4,000 pieces respectively.

Inspector Earnest selected a sample of 12 envelopes with the questionable stamps and sent them to the crime laboratory for analysis. In a report dated March 24, Laboratory Examiner S.C. Shimoda reported the postage stamps were, in fact, counterfeits. Several days previously Shimoda had given the inspector a preliminary verbal report stating the same. Now, knowing his judgment had been verified and these items did not constitute "mail," Inspector Earnest opened several of the envelopes. He discovered the enclosures were all identical pornographic solicitations involving bestiality, or sex between humans and animals.

Earnest filed reports of his investigation that would be used as a template in describing what occurred. He reported the initial discovery, and that since the date of the first seizure, an additional 5,200 envelopes were mailed at Anaheim, intercepted, and turned over to the Inspection Service. Some of these items it was found had postmarks from both Orange and Santa Ana, California. Based on this discovery, Inspector Earnest sent out a general warning to watch for and hold any suspicious mailings, and to notify the inspectors immediately if any were found. The recovered mailings were examined and it was found they were addressed to locations throughout the United States and even overseas. The return address was found to be a commercial mail drop named "Postal Express" in Anaheim.

On March 21, 1983, Inspector Earnest reviewed the "Application for Delivery of Mail through and agent" for the R.B. Company. This application had been filed on January 25, 1983, and was signed with the name Walton Ray Benton, whose identification information was listed as Texas driver's license number 8612110767; the Texas DMV reported this number was found to be invalid.

The operator of the mail drop described the applicant as a white male in his 40s or 50s, 5-foot-10-inches tall, medium build, clean shaven, gray medium-length hair, casually dressed, Texas accent, with no distinguishing features except for a scar on his chest that the subject said was due to open-heart surgery. Mrs. .... also stated that the subject picks up his mail once or twice a week, usually after the mail drop had been closed for the day.

Further investigation revealed two additional mail drops the subject was using in Las Vegas, NV. There also was one used in Los Angeles, and two others were found in Orange County. Only one of these mail drops was identified as still in use. It was located at 18932 Lemon Drive, Yorba, California. This business was known as the "Postal Annex," and was operated by ..... The operator was interviewed on March 22, and that application was reviewed. The mailbox had been rented on December 20, 1982, and again the applications had been signed Walton Ray Benton. The same phony address and identification was used as on the previous applications. Mr. .... Description of the subject was essentially the same as the one given by Mrs. ....

On March 22, 1983, Inspector Earnest contacted Detective Steve Walker of the Anaheim Police Department. He found that Detective Walker was presently working a pornography case involving bestiality and had identified a suspect he knew as Walton Ray Benton. The detective had no additional information from what the inspector had already obtained, but he did give the inspector the names of two Los Angeles Police Department detectives. Bob Peters and Frank Gilb had been working a case on the same suspect for approximately one year. They had run 24-hour stakeouts on other mail drops they had identified and had located him on two occasions. When the detectives tried to follow him, both times the subject shook off their surveillance by using diversionary tactics in his vehicle.

The vehicle the subject had been driving was a 1971, brown, 4-door AMC Ambassador with Texas license plate HUX707. This license plate was registered to William T. Samon, 2406 West Main, Grand Prairie, Texas. The description of Samon in Texas did not match that of the individual they were investigating in California. The LAPD ran the name Walton Ray Benton through the Texas DMV and located a valid driver's license and a photograph for Walton Ray Benton. The address listed was 3208 El Corto, Grand Prairie, Texas.

When the license photographs were shown to operators of the different mail drops, each definitely said this was not the person who rented a post office box at their respective facilities. Also, Detectives Peters and Gilb, who had seen the suspect, stated that the pictures did not match the individual they had under surveillance. The case continued, and neither the inspectors or the detectives had any idea of the true identity of the offender.

Using normal police techniques to locate their suspect, they reached out to informants. The information they got back was good. It appeared this individual had shorted one of the porno photo labs for at least $7,000. The lab operator was looking for the same person the detectives were, only in his case he wanted to kill him. Every attempt to learn the identity of their suspect was still being frustrated. In their reports it was noted every attempt they made to follow this person had been frustrated with his diversionary driving.

One lead the investigators still had was the "Postal Express," an active mail drop. On April 6, the inspectors obtained a court order that authorized the placement of an electronic tracking device on the suspect's vehicle when he next visited the facility. Postal Inspector Russ Maybre, from the Western Region Technical Support office, brought an AT-3 beeper unit and two Wackenhut tracking units to Los Angeles. The plan was to slip a beeper unit into mail the suspect would be picking up. The beeper gives the agents a constant signal within a limited range. With the Wackenhut, this is an actual tracking device and if it worked it would display the suspect vehicle's route of travel in real time.

On April 9, at approximately 9:25 p.m., the suspect was observed arriving at the "Postal Express." He was observed driving the vehicle that had been previously identified. Unfortunately, there was insufficient time to attach the tracking device; so once again, they tried simply to follow the man. Once again, the individual proved that he was a master of evasive driving. He pulled a U-turn when going down a residential street that did not lose the tail, but then when he got onto the Santa Ana freeway he had stopped in the emergency lane. Agents continued to the next exit thinking they would pick him up there – only he never appeared. He must have pulled a U-turn on the freeway and again blew off the tail.

Stymied again, all the agents could do was wait for developments. Then on April 11, it was discovered that approximately 4,000 pieces of mail with counterfeit stamps were dropped off at the Anaheim Post Office. Inspector Earnest obtained a sample of the mailing and then let the rest go on in order to allay any suspicion. The return address on the envelopes was identified as R.B. Company, 1626 North Wilcox, Suite 206, Hollywood, California 90028. This was a new mail drop and the identification provided on the new PS Form 1583 was again determined to be invalid. On the same date, Detective Peters received an unsolicited mailing at one of the addresses he had set up for test purposes in routine pornography investigations. This time, the content of the mailing was a solicitation selling child pornography. The return address on this mailing was for L.A. Stuart at 8033 Sunset Boulevard, Hollywood, California 90046. When this address was checked it was found to be another commercial mail drop. From both the handwriting on the application form and the physical description of the renter, it appeared that the person using the name Walton Ray Benton was the same person using the name Lyle A. Stuart.

In Los Angeles on April 14, 1983, Postal Inspector Percy Alexander was notified of this investigation. He had also been working a pornography complaint believed to involve the same subject. The person involved was using the company name of C.F. Limited. It was soon learned that other company names being used were Canine Fantasies, Kings and Queens, R.B. Company, and again L.A. Stuart Company.

Unfortunately, Inspector Alexander had little new information to add to the case file. On April 15, 1983, Inspector Earnest reached out to contact Postal Inspector Lynn Clendenin in Dallas, Texas. He had also been working a pornography case regarding a subject using the name Canine Fantasies. That case had been closed when his suspect had moved to Los Angeles. Inspector Clendenin stated that Detectives Doug Elder of the Houston Police Department, and Mike Ozga, Dallas Police Department, were also working pornography cases regarding this subject. Again, none of these investigations appeared to have any significant information to contribute.

Planning how to go at this again, Inspector Earnest met with Detectives Peters and Gilb at their office to devise a new plan to take this person down. Beginning on Saturday, April 23, they planned to start a 24-hour surveillance on the mail drop located on North Wilcox. The original participants were going to be the inspectors and officers from the LAPD. At the last minute the Secret Service, who originally had declined to participate, also decided they wanted in.

Detective Peters had received permission from his superiors for an extensive surveillance. The plan was to use a black and white unit to stop the suspect's car when he arrived at the mail facility. While the driver was distracted, an electronic tracking device would be attached to his vehicle. They even had an air unit on standby. Secret Service Agent Chuck Brewster represented his agency and interjected that in his experience when pornography and counterfeiting were found together almost always you would also find the presence of organized crime.

This time the plan appeared to be working. When the suspect arrived to pick up his mail, a unit swooped down to make a "car stop" and the tracking device was slapped on his car. Still, this was an individual who was paranoid to the extreme. Shortly after leaving the mail drop he once again blew the surveillance, and disappeared.

In the long run it was the tracking device that came to the agent's salvation. While on a routine patrol a few nights later, a police helicopter picked up the beeper signal. Once notified of the general area, agents and the detectives going block by block were able to track the vehicle down. Now, with a location, they were able to zero in on the suspect. On April 29, he was picked up, identified, and charged in federal court. He would be charged with the counterfeiting of $1.37 million in phony flag over the Supreme Court regular-issue stamps.

LAPD sources would publicly state that approximately 250,000 of these stamps had been used in the mail. These unsolicited mailings had been widespread, going to addresses in all parts of the country. Another discovery made was that an unknown amount of these counterfeit stamps had also been sold to local businesses for their use as well.

The person who had been leading the authorities on this wild chase was finally identified as James Croy of Huntington Beach, California. He was hardly new to the world of crime. He had an outstanding federal fugitive warrant out of Macon, Georgia. Still, before he was turned over to the U.S. Marshalls, he cooperated and led the agents to a second location where his partner in crime was arrested. This person was Monte Hailer, who operated the Godspeed Printing Company. In the search that followed, agents found not only stamps, but also $86,000 worth of counterfeit currency in various denominations.

Even though the Secret Service had been Johnny-come-lately to the investigation, when the arrest went down, they promptly called a press conference and claimed credit for the arrests and seizures. At the Secret Service office they put on a dog-and-pony show for the media, displaying examples of the seized items. Ashley G. Williams, the head of the Los Angeles office of the Secret Service stated, "This is the largest single seizure of counterfeit postage stamps in the United States."

The stamps that were displayed for the press were described as being of poor quality. The sizing was wrong and the perforations were pitiful. A contrary view was given by the Director of the West Coast Inspection Service crime laboratory; he stated the stamps produced in this case were not all that bad. After all, they had been flowing through the mail for some time. Apparently the printer had used two different varieties of paper, one was gummed and the other was not. The stamp's sizing was a reasonable match to the original. They were printed in "ninety" or ninety-nine stamps per sheet format. Obviously they were being printed as a private contract and not designed to be sold on the street. The perforations on at least some of the items were identified as being 9mm rather than 11mm as found on the legitimate item. On my own Stanley Gibbons Instanta perforation gauge the stamp was found to be 12mm. This was an offset printing. Another obvious identification characteristic was ink breaks in the stripes in the flag. Documentation revealed that in just six months of operation, Croy took in over $250,000. Apparently someone was buying his products, and that is frightening.

In recognition of their attentiveness and dedication to their work, the two postal employees responsible for the discovery of this case each received a $500 achievement award and letters of commendation from Eric G. Larson, the acting Inspector in Charge of the Los Angeles Inspection Service Division.

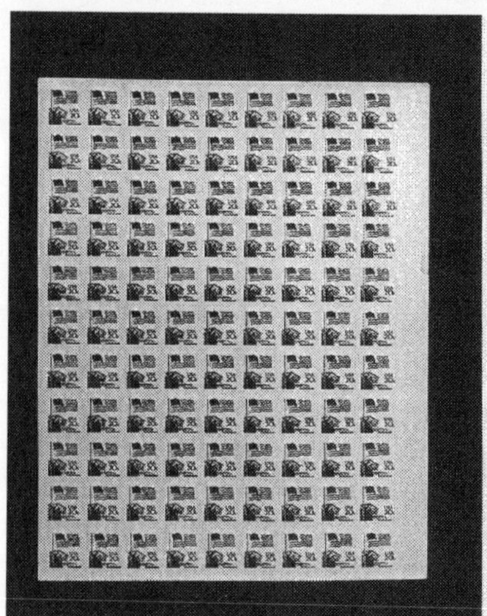

Illustration of stamp sheet and close-up of stamp block

Counterfeit 20-cent flag over Supreme Court building, showing one in Coil, left, and one regular issue. Note the perforation differences indicating two

Stamp Destruction and Discounted Postage!

Both postal and Inspection Service management have been reluctant to acknowledge that there was a problem with stamp revenue protection. The emphasis has always been to move the mail, not to look at it. Year after year reports came into Washington reporting stamp counterfeiting and postage meter problems. A straw that would at least temporarily break the back of denial involved, of all things, stamp destruction. The establishment mindset was that of the "average honest man." The thought was that yes, there would always be some who might cheat or even steal to save a few pennies, but the average honest person would not succumb to that temptation. Reality would prove this philosophy wrong.

When the cost of postage began to escalate, the Postal Service was faced with a dilemma. Suddenly, they had hundreds of millions of 13-cent stamps no longer wanted by the public. The solution provided was simple: send this unwanted stamp stock to your local incinerator. At Louisville, Ky., this created another dilemma when $1.5 million in stamps had been sent to a local incinerator, and only one-third of the stamps were destroyed. The missing stamps would hit the streets as discounted postage. Then in 1983, the same problem was discovered in New York.

Millions of dollars in postage stock had been brought to the Brooklyn incinerator with a heavy security escort. Inspectors and postal employees would watch this stamp stock as it was placed on conveyer belts and disappear into the facility. The only problem was that as this material was going down the conveyer, before it hit the flames, there were sanitation employees who would take some of it off the belt. The inspectors were tipped off that something wasn't working, not by observing what occurred, but rather when some stamps began to blow out the chimney. A number of sanitation employees would eventually be prosecuted as well as a number of East Coast stamp dealers who knowingly were selling this material as discounted postage.

Still, the argument raged in Washington about the extent of the revenue problem and what could be done. In the spring of

1983, at Inspection Service headquarters, the Criminal Investigation Division began studying the effectiveness of its revenue protection efforts. The concern was evident about the number and complexity of counterfeiting cases discovered, as well as reuse of postage by the public, and the fencing of legitimate postage stolen in robberies and burglaries. Then added to the mix was a report from the Office of Audit that there was insufficient accountability of postage meters; many were reported lost or stolen. Tens of thousands of meter machines could not be accounted for by either the Postal Service or the meter manufacturers.

The conclusion drawn was that while the Inspection Service was very successful when they discovered, and then investigated revenue cases, all of their efforts were basically reactive rather than proactive. There was no program to identify illegal operations before they resulted in significant revenue loss. There was no way to even judge what the extent of revenue loss was. In January of 1984, a number of inspectors were brought into the Career Development Branch – the Inspection Service training facility. The idea was that these inspectors would go back to their respective divisions to identify if problems existed in their area.

The first thing the inspectors tripped over was the low-hanging fruit. It was called reuse of postage. Probably every one of us has received personal mail where the stamp had not been cancelled. At one time or another, a large percentage of the public has clipped that stamp off and put it on another piece of mail. The thinking was, well the stamp was not cancelled, so it must still be good to use again. When this is an individual citizen this may be an aggravation, but hardly a problem. But what about when this becomes a cottage industry?

What was uncovered was that a stamp reuse industry had grown up all across the country. We are not talking about the sale of a few washed stamps here and there, but sales that ranged from thousands to hundreds of thousands of stamps. The individuals executing this dastardly crime mostly were retired or semi-retired stamp collectors who in many cases were simply keeping themselves occupied. If you are laughing about this, simply go back to any stamp publication in the 1970s and look at the ads. In every issue you will find numerous solicitations to either buy or sell ungummed, unused postage. What nobody mentioned was that there simply was no legitimate source for ungummed, unused postage. At least not in any quantity.

Basically this was a monster that the Post Office created. Every day hundreds of thousands of pieces of mail would get delivered without the stamp having been cancelled by the Post Office. The private citizen seeing this would think, why not? The common thinking was, well, if it has not been cancelled it must still be good. A cottage industry sprang up that was costing the postal service hundreds of thousands.

Was this activity significant? In a two-year period there were in excess of two hundred and fifty jacketed cases for investigation. In 1984 more than $13 million washed stamps were seized. In 1985 this number would exceed 54 million stamps with a face value of $11 million. In every instance where the seizure of washed stamps occurred, evidence had been obtained that proved the operator was knowingly selling used stamps with the intent that they be used again in the mail. In many cases a copy of the criminal code was found right at hand. A few examples:

Drake, Colorado – One Million Washed Stamps Seized

On September 27, 1984, inspectors executed a federal search warrant and seized approximately one million ungummed, previously used U.S. postage stamps and approximately 2.5 million canceled postage stamps. Also seized were extensive business records pertaining to the suspect's enterprises. He was engaged in a stamp brokerage and was not personally washing stamps. Information from this and other contraband postage cases linked him as a primary supplier of canceled stamps to a stamp washing ring in Kentucky, the subject of a similar search.

Merriam, Kansas – Contraband Postage Dealer Indicted

On July 17, 1984, a federal search warrant was executed on a residence in Merriam. The warrant was authorized after several test purchases and undercover buys of washed stamps. The suspect admitted to undercover postal inspectors that his business grossed approximately $15,300 per month in washed stamp sales. Approximately 1.5 million canceled stamps and several thousand washed stamps packaged for resale were seized at his residence. On April 9, 1985, a Federal Grand Jury in Kansas City returned a four-count felony indictment charging the suspect with possession and dealing in altered obligations of the United States that were washed U.S. postage stamps.

Spokane, Washington – Five Million Stamps Recovered

On April 11, 1984, a two-month undercover investigation relating to a stamp-washing operation resulted in the execution of a search warrant on a Spokane residence. A total of 91 large cardboard boxes containing an estimated five million used postage stamps and envelopes were seized. On May 21, 1984, two defendants were indicted by a Federal Grand Jury, and on July 27, they were sentenced to two years probation.

Cincinnati, Ohio – Fifty Million Stamps Seized

On February 11, 1985, a search warrant was executed on a business office in Cincinnati. Approximately 50 million stamps and stamps on paper, all bearing canceled U.S. postage marks over 100,000 washed stamps of mixed denominations with a face value of $15,000 were ready for resale; and business records and other correspondence relating to a nationwide discount postage selling operation were seized. Probable cause for the search warrant was based on electronic surveillance and the purchase of $1,000 face value of washed postage for $750 by an undercover postal inspector.

St. Louis, Missouri – Contraband Postage Seized

A search warrant was executed on February 12, 1985, at a residence in St. Louis. Approximately 42,000 washed stamps and nearly 2,230,500 unwashed, loose stamps were seized. Probable cause for the search warrant was based in part on purchases of washed postage that were made by an undercover postal inspector on three separate occasions.

The aforementioned incidents were just a sample of cases reported in a summation of activities published by National Headquarters. It gives just a bird's-eye view of what was discovered occurring all across the United States. You might think of it as death by a thousand cuts. In dealing with it the intent was not to harass and prosecute a bunch of nice old men and women who were simply keeping themselves occupied while making a few bucks. In most cases the idea was simply getting their attention and putting them on notice to knock it off. In a couple of incidents the individuals simply refused to get the message. In those cases after about the third visit from agents there was no choice but to take them off in handcuffs for prosecution.

Did this sudden attention end this activity? Not hardly. It still goes on, but nowhere to the same degree as before. One of the last cases I worked before leaving the service involved a senior citizen outside of St. Paul. After a number of stamp buys, and determining that the items he was selling had seen prior postal use, a search warrant was served on his house. What was found went beyond anyone's expectations. In getting his raw material he had created a monster. Contracting with a large mail receiver he told them he could hall away their trash incoming mail envelopes. First he filled his garage, then his house, then five outbuildings on his property. He even rented a barn from a neighbor. When the inspectors showed up, the happiest person was his wife. We filled 18 semi trailers to haul this material away.[48]

For anyone who may have questions about what the government was doing here, the Justice Department has consistently ruled that "knowingly reusing of stamps that have previously seen postal use, whether those items are cancelled or not, represents counterfeiting offenses." In the 1980s a large percentage of stamps were going through the process without being cancelled. In at least one instance it was found that a postal supervisor had actually bypassed the canceling of stamps to speed up the delivery of mail. After all, supervisors were graded by meeting delivery criteria, not on revenue protection. The postal bureaucracy has consistently been the greatest obstruction to the protection of postal revenue.

The Postage Meter

In all of the time I was either investigating or researching counterfeiting, there was one area I looked upon with dread. This was

48 After about a month the Post Office wanted their trailers back. A local university had an in-house incinerator they used to generate power and heat. I figured I heated the school for about a week.

the meter machine. I had soon concluded that if individuals would go to the effort of counterfeiting a stamp, surely you could exploit this simple machine.

On December 10, 1920, the United States Post Office Department had authorized the use of meters to prepay mailing expenses. These machines were designed so that a meter impression could be used rather than a postage stamp. If you had tried to design a way to be ripped off, it would be hard to devise an easier system just waiting to be exploited. A few cases previously presented should have told someone we could have a problem here. The Contraband Postage Program would finally expose the problem.

Nobody expected to find the nightmare they did. It started innocently enough. It was known that on occasion meters would malfunction. It was called jackpotting. You would exhaust the postage you had purchased, and the machine instead of locking out would roll over and continue to issue postage. The way something like this would normally be caught is the postal requirement that periodically meters have to be brought in to the Post Office for either more postage or inspection. The only problem with that is some Post Offices were better than others. Then it was discovered that some individuals had made the same discovery that Bernard Abelson had and were manually resetting the machines themselves.

Eventually people would conclude why bother. I have this meter and I will just call it in as lost or stolen. Then I can knock the seals off and put in all the postage I ever wanted. When the Inspection Service finally tumbled onto what was going on, they began to identify businesses that lo and behold were still using meters that the Post Office showed as out of service, or rather reported as lost or stolen. Not surprisingly many of these users were very large mail preparation/pre-sort businesses. One facility was visited that served the New York area included many government offices. Somewhere in the area of 32 manipulated meters were found up in a false ceiling. This was just one of many cases that were discovered. Pitney Bowes was finally forced to account for their mechanical meters. Imagine the joy in Washington when it was discovered that somewhere between 20,000 to 40,000 meters were listed in our records that no longer could be accounted for. Free postage anyone?

These reports were not received with overwhelming approval as obviously the interests of both users and manufacturers of postage meters were well represented on Capitol Hill. The final straw may have been a report on September 26, 1996, generated by the Government Accountability Office. This report was addressed to David Pryor, the ranking minority member of the Subcommittee on Post Office and Civil Service. It identified that the problem with fraudulent meter use could be as high as $100 million annually. This was a low-ball estimate. Faced with the facts and figures given to Congress, the situation became so serious that the Postmaster General threatened to eliminate the use of meters unless corrective action was taken by the respective companies.

If one tried to fully document the extent of meter fraud discovered, that would constitute a book all by itself. The inspectors and the GAO had done exactly what they were meant to do – to protect the revenue of the government. Finally, they got someone to pay attention to what they had been discovering and reporting for years.

Or at least I thought that when I retired.

7

Back to Stamps

One of the last counterfeit stamp cases I physically played a part in was in 1985, in Detroit. This was strictly in an advisory capacity, and I was simply there as an extra body. The case was very capably handled by inspectors from the Detroit Division. The task force leader was Inspector John E. Hemphill. When his team developed information that a local resident was moving into the stamp business they moved in to find out if this was true.

In a four-month joint investigation with the Secret Service, agents were able to first identify, and then develop a business relationship with the target of the investigation. This was Isaiah Prince III, a black male, DOB 07/18/45. Contact was maintained with Prince while he worked his way through his printing problems. The primary target of his attention was the type "D" nondenominational stamp. When he began to run them off his press, a purchase of several thousand of these items was negotiated for by Inspector D. Ervin who had been working with Prince in an undercover capacity.

At one point Prince complained to the undercover agent he was having problems finding an adequate perforator to handle the quantity of stamps he wished to run off. The agent assured him this was not a problem; Ervin said he could handle this himself. Unbeknownst to Prince, that night the counterfeit stamps were on a flight to Washington, D.C. Taken to the Bureau of Engraving and Printing, they were perforated on the same machines the government used for the production of their own legitimate issue stamps.

When later the next day they were returned to Prince he oohed and aahed over the quality of the perforations. A deal was soon struck where Prince would print a large quantity of stamps for the agent. More than enough probable cause had been developed for a search of the suspected printing facility. The warrant was executed on Prince's business, MTM Printing and Duplicating, located at 18264 Wyoming Street in Detroit, Michigan. Items seized included cameras, an offset press, plate making and numbering machines. Also discovered were counterfeit prescription pads, state of Michigan driver's license applications, birth certificates, Social Security cards, City of Detroit building inspection certificates, along with proofs of U.S. postage stamps and U.S. Treasury bills in denominations of $1, $5, $10, $20, and $50.

None of the postage stamps printed reached the point of being marketed to the public.

In 1985, I left Chicago behind for another assignment, and mostly I was no longer involved in postal counterfeiting cases. This did not mean this type of criminal activity had ended, but it seemed to be changing. Organized crime in the United States had been very seriously under attack by the FBI, and the structure and discipline that had been there since the 1930s was disappearing. "The Mob" would play a diminishing role in this activity. Still, counterfeit postage cases would be found.

In the spring of 1985, a homegrown attempt was discovered in Lubbock, Texas. This was a Secret Service investigation that was worked by Agent William Morrow. It began like many currency cases do. Agent Morrow was following up on the report of a woman who passed a counterfeit $50 Federal Reserve note at a local J.C. Penney store.

When questioned, the woman claimed to have no idea that the bill she passed was bogus, and then a search of her vehicle disclosed another. She was soon identified as passing an identical bill at another location. Still, she stayed with her story. She claimed to have received the money from the sale of a car. That story would soon fall apart when Morrow found $6,165 in counterfeit $1, $5, and $50s in a milk container at her house. How Morrow talked his way into her residence I have no idea, but it was her downfall. Finally, she would confess and identify her husband as the printer, and oh yes, the counterfeit plant used to print the bills was in the basement. Counterfeit currency totaling $161,753 would be found in the house. Morrow also discovered $8,613 in counterfeit "D" stamps in the basement as well.

None of the stamp sheets had as yet been perforated and the quality of the printing was described as "poor." It is believed that none of these stamps were ever distributed or used, but the authorities didn't know that for sure. The nondenominational type "D" stamp was hardly a pictorial or technological wonder, and it was at this time colored photocopy machines began to hit the market. On a regular basis, photocopied stamps would be identified flowing through the mail, so as poor as the Lubbock "D" stamps may have been, there would be no difficulty in their being used either.

I am sure that postal counterfeiting did not go away, but for some reason there seemed to be about a 10-year break in any significant cases that I am aware of. With other responsibilities on a day-to-day basis, I had not kept up with postage fraud.[49] Then, when I did start to look for counterfeit cases again, I no longer had access to inside information. Years later when I once again sat down and seriously started to look again, I discovered something had happened. It appeared the Post Office was again under attack. Actually the cases had not gone away. It was simply that I was not looking for them.

Los Angeles, December 1997

On December 16, 1997, Los Angeles Division postal inspectors executed a federal search warrant on Valley Advertising in Fountain Valley, California. The purpose of this visit was to locate counterfeit postage stamps and the equipment used to create counterfeit postage stamps. This search had not been pulled out of someone's imagination. In mid October, the Los Angeles Division received information from postal management regarding the alleged use of counterfeit postage stamps on numerous envelopes being discovered in the mail at the Santa Ana and Anaheim facilities. A sampling of the suspicious mail was examined and inspectors verified that the stamps being used were in fact counterfeit 32-cent yellow rose stamps.

Subsequent investigation and interviews with postal personnel disclosed that suspect mail being "Returned to Sender" had an address located on Buttonwood Street in Fountain Valley, California. Watching this business, inspectors determined this business was depositing their outgoing mail in a collection box located near the Buttonwood address.

A search warrant for the suspected address was obtained and executed on December 16, 1997. Items seized during the search

49 One of my ongoing nightmares was security of gold shipments. Every week about 10 armed guards would bring about $20 million in gold to the back dock of one of my Post Offices. We would then put it in a truck and one postal employee would drive it about 100 miles on back country roads to the mail processing center. Can you say disaster waiting to happen?

included a computer, scanner, printer, paper edging scissors, glue, and matte coated paper. All items seized were believed to be used in the creation of counterfeit postage. Further items seized included 31 sheets of paper bearing approximately 900 counterfeit 32-cent yellow rose stamps with a value of $280. This was not a multi-million dollar operation.

Daniel Kahn, the owner/operator of Valley Advertising, showed inspectors the method he used to produce the counterfeit postage. In the presence of inspectors, he even ran off a sample sheet of counterfeit postage. During the interview, Kahn told inspectors he would scan a single yellow rose stamp, then multiply the stamp image using his computer. The final result was a sheet of counterfeit stamps. This is basically the same methodology used to produce plates to print currency. The only difference was that he was using a computer rather than a camera. Perforator– who needed a perforator? He stated he simply purchased an edging scissor at an art store.

To see if this scheme would work, Kahn said he had first "test-mailed" a letter bearing a counterfeit stamp to himself. When this item was successfully delivered he knew his scheme could pass through the mail without detection. To throw off any attempt by the authorities to trace the stamps back to himself he further stated he deposited his mailings at various locations and on various dates. Kahn admitted to using approximately 800 of the counterfeit stamps that totaled approximately $260. Kahn further admitted that prior to the search he had intended to use the remaining 400 sheets of matte paper he had on hand to make more stamps.

Before I retired from the Inspection Service, I did have a similar case. It was in, of all places, Sioux Falls, South Dakota. Adding insult to injury, the individual involved had used the color copier in the lobby of the Post Office to make his photocopies.

In the world of crime, historically, the counterfeiter was considered to be almost royalty. Before the age of computers this was a highly skilled occupation, the practitioners of which were always in demand. You had to possess printing skill, cameras, plate-making equipment, and a working knowledge of inks and paper. This was not a skill that normally a person would pick up in an afternoon of just fooling around.

The computer, scanner, and quality color printers changed this world. A thorn in the side of the Secret Service today is that about 80 plus percent of the currency manufactured in the United States is made by some novice, such as a high school kid in his bedroom. Stamps obviously would not escape this notice as well. What has really been a thorn in the side of the Secret Service are the professional counterfeiters who have also learned how to use computers and scanners.

On page 2 of the July 20, 1998, issue of *Linn's Stamp News* was the headline; "Fake 32-cent Porch found in Mixture." William Menker related how Terry Holdridge of Iowa Stamp and Coins discovered what he believed to be an obviously bogus stamp in a mixture he had purchased from a stamp soaker.

This item had been produced from either a color copier or on an ink-jet printer. Menker described the quality of this stamp as poor at best. "There was no trace of phosphorescent tagging, and again the counterfeit appeared to have been cut by pinking shears." It can at least be said that this item had been made to look like a coil stamp as both the top and bottom edges were cut with straight edges. This stamp had been postally used as demonstrated by the cancellation. The general consensus in the philatelic world was that it would be spotted in an instant. The obvious question then is why had this item gone so easily through the system? The answer unfortunately is simple. Nobody in the Post Office really looks at postage, or in most cases even feels they are responsible for revenue protection.

If you are a collector looking for counterfeits, there are a few places you can go. Commonly, they appear in auctions identified as such. Also, if you have a relationship with an established stamp dealer, sometimes you can obtain these items at a reasonable price. The reason I stress "having a relationship" is because if you are an unknown buyer there just may be a reluctance to sell a stranger such items. Call it a hangover from the Jacob Hoffman prosecution in the 1930s.

There are also individuals who have turned their quest into a treasure hunt. Collectors frequently have discovered counterfeits in relatively inexpensive stamp mixtures. You never know what may be found. A great resource for the collector to aid in the identification of counterfeits is the new Scott Specialized catalogue for 2013. For the first time a supplemental section was included that offered colored illustrations and stamp descriptions to aid in the identification of postal counterfeits.[50]

No sooner do I say no postal employees look at stamps, and another instance pops up that most likely was discovered due to an attentive postal employee. An Inspection Service communication was found from the Memphis Division going to Washington reporting their action against one counterfeit postage operation. It also gave evidence that the Inspection Service was following up with the Contraband Postage Program as had been planned and was giving attention to revenue security. Again, this case would involve the utilization of computers to generate bogus postage. It was dated January 6, 1998.

Inspectors from Memphis and other divisions executed a search warrant at 8007 Trinity Mills Road in Cordova, Tennessee. This was the residence of Dale Stump and was also the business address of R&B Service, Inc. This was a stamp-vending business that was solely owned and operated by Stump, one he had operated for eight years. Stump owned and had in place approximately 300 stamp-vending machines, most of which were located in convenience stores throughout the Memphis area.

It was reported that the search warrant had been obtained based on information provided by postal employees who identified suspected counterfeit stamps affixed to mail rejected by the facer/canceller machines in their mail processing center. Information had also come in from a postal customer who had purchased stamps out of one of Stump's machines. This observant customer reported he believed the stamps being dispensed were counterfeit. To follow these reports up inspectors made their own test purchases and verified that in their opinion counterfeit stamps were being sold using these machines. To officially confirm this judgment the stamps purchased were submitted to the Memphis Forensic Laboratory. As expected they were declared as counterfeit.

Based on the evidence developed, a search was executed, and after Stump signed a warning and waiver form, he was interviewed.

---

50 This was primarily compiled by John Hotchner to whom the stamp world owes a debt of thanks.

Confronting reality, he provided a written sworn statement. He admitted to using a color copier to produce counterfeit 32-cent Utah and Tennessee stamps for sale out of his vending machines. He acknowledged that he began making his own stamps in early December of 1997. The idea came from watching a show that described how to reproduce items using a computer, scanner and laser color printer. Supporting his statement, records seized showed he purchased his color copier on December 5, 1997. Stump indicated there was no particular reason he picked on the Utah and Tennessee sheets for reproduction. They simply were convenient.

Stump stated he began his counterfeiting adventure simply in an effort to pay off debts resulting from gambling losses at local casinos. He probably figured he had more to worry about from casino owners than he did the government. He claimed he had only made approximately $1,600 from the sale of his computer-generated stamps. From information seized during the search, it was estimated that actually somewhere between 10,000 and 15,000 32-cent stamps valued at between $3,200 and $4,800 had been produced.

Stump was very cooperative in his interviews. He even agreed to demonstrate to the inspectors his method for printing his stamps. As both evidence, and possibly even as a training aid, the inspectors videotaped Stump producing a sheet of fifty 32-cent stamps. He simply used the gummed paper in his paper tray and a good sheet of 32-cent Utah stamps. After the copies were produced he sprayed the printed side with a "clear gloss" aerosol spray to harden the ink and to prevent smudging. This also provided a more glossy appearance. He then proceeded to demonstrate his technique for cutting, perforating and preparing single counterfeit stamps for sale in his machines. Obviously this was not a multimillion dollar operation, but it illustrated the susceptibility of postal revenue to attack by just about anyone with a computer and printer.

The agents seized an HP 120 color copier, $4,843.60 in coins, 27 stamp-vending machines, a coin counter/sorter, miscellaneous business records, and other items used in the counterfeiting of these stamps. Also seized was a quantity of legitimate stamps and an estimated 1,200 counterfeit stamps. Stump provided a listing of a number of businesses where his machines were located and those machines were also seized. An inventory of their contents disclosed $2,296.35 in coins, and $2,480.72 in legitimate stamps and $315.20 in other suspected counterfeit stamps.

An administrative seizure warrant was filed for all R&B vending machines in the Western District of Tennessee (approximately 225). The total of counterfeit stamps seized amounted to $1,234.88. It was estimated that somewhere between 10,000 and 15,000 in counterfeit stamps had been produced. The question that really begs to be asked is how many others may have decided to also make their own stamps?

And then there is old school. This is a story that was reported in the U.S. Postal *Inspection Service Bulletin* in December of 1999, and also by Wayne Youngblood in the June 22, 1998, issue of *Stamp Collector*. In September of 1997, an alert postal clerk by the name of Wayne Meyers working as a forwarding clerk in Phoenix, Arizona noted an irregularity on a flat-sized envelope. Wayne was a stamp collector, so he paid attention to stamps. In this case there were two 46-cent Ruth Benedict stamps on this envelope that he thought simply did not look right. He stated that the color seemed to be a bit off, and the stamps appeared to have a flat appearance. Meyers called this to the attention of his supervisor who in turn contacted the local Postal Inspectors.

The subject envelope had been mailed from Wisconsin so everything was referred to the Milwaukee office for investigation. It ended up on the desk of Postal Inspector Patti Peters who had the contraband postage assignment. Peters performed the same field test that inspectors in Arizona did – she checked the phosphor tagging with a black light. The suspect stamps had no phosphor tagging, a tell-tale sign this was a counterfeit. Verification would be supplied by Richard French, a forensic examiner at the National Laboratory in Dulles, Virginia.

The return address on the envelope was Infinity Fulfillment Center, American Freeway, 100 Wisconsin, 53811-0552. This zip code belonged to Hazel Green, a small southwestern Wisconsin community with a population of only 1,200. The envelope may not have had a street address, but when asked, Lorie Leibfried, the postmaster, knew exactly who the mailer was. His name was John (Jack) Bastian, a printer who also was locally known for operating various get-rich-quick schemes.

Postmaster Leibfried had noticed that Bastian on a daily basis had been buying 55-cent and 46-cent stamps, and then suddenly stopped. He had been buying so many of these stamps that to meet his needs it had been necessary for the postmaster to make a special requisition. Then, when these purchases suddenly stopped, the local Post Office was suddenly stuck with a large quantity of these items. Being concerned, she asked Bastian what was going on. His response was that his business partner, Doug Burdick, was now "taking care of it."

Through checking business records, Inspector Peters determined Bastian had remodeled his house and set up a printing business in the back. When she checked the house out, Peters saw a sign on the back door, "Infinity, Inc." Another inspector, Brian Haraway, was sent into the residence in an undercover capacity to request information on his business. "I heard I could make some money," he told Bastian, and requested more information on how this would work.

Bastian promptly mailed Haraway his literature, which turned out to be a multilevel marketing program. He was also selling a video along with the basic information that described how one purportedly would make money using his scheme. When Haraway received this information it was noted that the postage on these items had been paid for using six 46-cent Ruth Benedict stamps plus a 32-cent stamp. The Benedict stamps were again found to be counterfeit. Establishing probable cause for a search warrant, the inspectors had Bastian's residence under surveillance. One night he was observed leaving and was followed to Dubuque, Iowa, where he was observed dropping off a plastic tub on the Post Office back dock. The inspectors verified the contents as being his mailings, which again utilized counterfeit stamps. Obviously Bastian was taking steps to avoid the prying eyes of his local postmaster back in Hazel Green.

When Bastian put his trash out on the curb, the inspectors moved in and grabbed it. In the trash, Inspector Peters found printing waste, namely the remnants of torn 46-cent Benedict stamps. There were also numerous strips of white paper that appeared to have the imprint of perforations. The stamp fragments were checked for phosphor tagging and again there was no evidence of tagging. At this point, it did not take a rocket scientist to conclude the location of the counterfeit plant had been pinned down.

Enough evidence had been developed to support a search warrant of Bastian's house, and the attached printing shop. At 8:00 a.m. October 29, 1997, Peters and other inspectors from the Milwaukee office accompanied by uniformed officers from the Hazel Green Police Department knocked on Bastian's door. When nobody answered, they entered and found him working on his computer in a back room. Initially Bastian exuded anger with the appearance of the agents, but the wind went out of his sails when he read the warrant.

Inspector Peters explained the facts of life to him, and after a few moments of contemplation he gave up any pretext of ignorance. He began to answer their questions.

"Why did you choose the Ruth Benedicts?"

His answer: "Red ink is easier to reproduce than any other color. It's closer to black."

The inspectors gave him a break to gather his thoughts and think things over. Then Peters asked him: "Do you want to keep talking?"

Bastian answered, "Big time, I want to get it off my chest."

It is always nice to have a confession, but in this case it was hardly a necessity. In their search the inspectors had found the plates and negatives for the counterfeit stamps, reams of gummed paper, and homemade perforator, a glue roller and, oh yes, 7,600 counterfeit stamps affixed to 2,145 flat-sized envelopes. There was an additional 1,453 counterfeit stamps in various stages of completion.

Also found were business records. They showed that Bastian had used 9,528 counterfeit stamps valued at $4,382.88. They had been sent out through the mail from August 6, 1997, until October 28 from Post Offices at Hazel Green, and Madison, Wisconsin; Irving Park, Illinois; Lafayette, Louisiana; and Dubuque, Iowa.

On April 2, 1998, Bastian was indicted by a Wisconsin Federal Grand Jury. He was charged with one count of Title 18 U.S. Code Section 501, stamp counterfeiting. Initially pleading not guilty, he changed his plea to guilty on June 3. On August 12, Bastian was sentenced to six months in prison to be followed with three years supervised probation. This was a downward diversion in the sentencing guidelines, and was based on his cooperation with the authorities. He served his sentence at the federal prison camp at

Duluth, Minnesota.

Also indicted were Douglas J. Burdick and Scott T. Cool. These men were charged with 18 U.S. Code 371 Conspiracy to counterfeit U.S. Postage stamps. It was Burdick who originally had suggested to Bastian that they could cut their postage cost if they made their own stamps. Scott Cool had also been involved in the execution of the scheme. Both men ultimately pleaded guilty to the lesser offense of 18 USC 641, public money, property or records, which was a lesser misdemeanor charge. The two men were each sentenced to two months probation and required to make restitution.

Bastian made this comment at his sentencing: "Counterfeiting of stamps was easy."

Things Get Confusing

Simply because what we knew of as "organized crime" has been driven underground, and stamp production may have changed, this does not mean that the problem with counterfeit postage would disappear. In a big way, new faces and new ways of doing things would make their presence felt. Now retired, this presented an increased challenge in trying to figure out what was going on, and who was doing it.

The first hint that a new and possibly greater challenge had appeared on the scene was found in the March 15, 2004, issue of *Linn's Stamp News.* This was a report by Charles Snee. He related how very good copies of the 2002, 37-cent flag stamp (Scott #3635) had been sold on eBay in January and February. The postal inspectors would verify that these ads were being placed on this website from both the East and West coasts.

Scott #3635 was just one variety of stamp design A2812. It was printed by the Banknote Corporation of America in booklet panes of 20 on each sheet. The die cut on the legitimate stamp is 11.3mm on 2, 3, or even 4 sides. It has a USPS microprint in the top red flag strip and a small 2002 year date in the lower right corner. The stamps on each sheet are mounted on card stock, the back side of which bears the USPS copyright, and identifies the stamp and price of $7.40.

Linn's first learned of the existence of this counterfeit from Dave

Cockrill, a part-time stamp dealer who lives in Washington State. According to Cockrill, a stamp dealer for whom he worked made a number of purchases from a seller on eBay. All of the items received had the plate No. B5555. These experienced dealers had no idea or suspicion that the items purchased and received were bogus. Not only was the quality of the printing good, but "the die cutting is dead on, nearly identical to the die cutting on genuine panes of stamps."

Cockrill resold some of these items to a Florida stamp dealer. He also sold items to other dealers who also specialized in coils. It was one of those latter individuals who soon called back with some disturbing information. "This PNC dealer called me and said to check the micro printing on the stamps." When he looked closely, he discovered the micro printing was missing. He stated that his first thought was "Oh, no."

Cockrill immediately notified both eBay and the postal inspectors. He was referred to Inspector Tony Robinson in Los Angeles, the assigned case agent. Although the details were never revealed, it was apparent the Inspection Service had been investigating this counterfeit stamp for some time. When *Linn's* contacted Inspector Robinson his comment to the paper was, "I want to give *Linn's* readers particulars of the case that can benefit them as stamp collectors without jeopardizing the integrity of the investigation. The trouble is, we're not at a point yet where we can do that." That statement was so much nicer than simply a cold "no" comment. The facts would ultimately show that a lot more was going on with this case than anyone not involved would imagine.

Following procedures, the Inspection Service took possession of all the counterfeit stamps they could identify. Or at least that is what was reported. Cockrill's dealer friend had to surrender 111 pads of stamps. Each stamp pad contained 100 panes of 20 stamps each, and each pad was individually wrapped. This stamp dealer was given a receipt for $82,140, the face value for the 222,000 stamps that were confiscated. The general conclusion put forward in *Linn's* was that with the volume of stamps discovered, their suspicion was that an unknown number of these items had, or soon would be, seeing use in the mail.

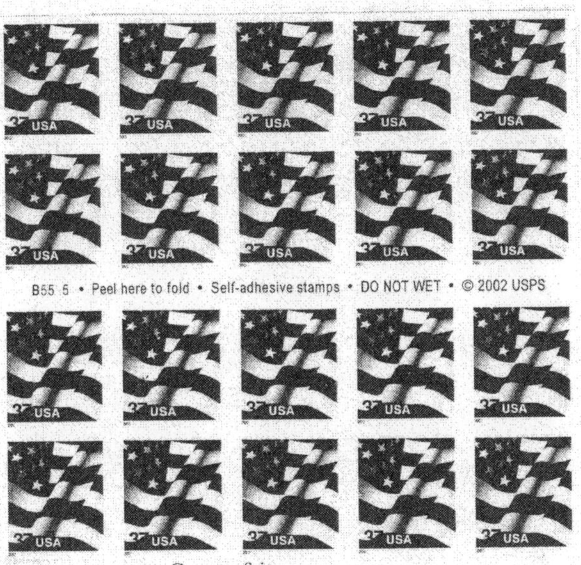

37-cent 2002 Scott #3635

Mailing envelope

New ground had been broken here. Most significantly the distribution problem had been solved. The counterfeiters had discovered the Internet, and counterfeit postage was being sold not at the price of legitimate postage, or as counterfeits, but as discounted postage. On the Internet the seller could be demanding a pricing level of 80 or even 90 percent of face value. These folks had also discovered the world of the stamp dealer who commonly deals in legitimate discounted postage. These items were being sold in large volume to dealers at 50 to 60 percent of face value. One stamp dealer acknowledged paying $50,000 for $100,000 worth of these items.

Commonly, discounted postage is older obsolete denominations now not in demand due to the escalation of stamp rates. In this case, the stamps being sold were the then current rate of postage. When a stranger walks into your business with a large amount of the then current stamps the normal suspicion is to suspect these items are stolen. When the inspectors asked dealers why they would buy this material and not report it as suspicious, a common refrain heard from stamp dealers was their complaint that the Postal Service does not talk to them. The Stamp Dealer Association has complained for years that if the Post Office suffers major stamp losses through either burglary or robbery, just maybe it would be a good idea if someone would tell them about it.

When he was interviewed by *Linn's,* Robinson was surprisingly forthcoming with information. He noted the inspectors had seen a marked increase in counterfeit stamp activity in just the last 12 months.

> With financial losses sometimes exceeding $100,000, counterfeit stamps are often produced within the continental United States; however, some counterfeits are produced abroad and then smuggled into port cities such as San Diego, Los Angeles, and San Francisco, and then transported and sold throughout the country.[51]
>
> Two methods of stamp transactions have been observed by postal inspectors. First, low-level fraudsters, under the guise of liquidating the stamp stock of a defunct company, are known to approach businesses offering to sell stamps to them at a discount.
>
> Second, counterfeit stamp transactions have also been facilitated by

51 I have a vague recollection of someone telling me about a ship that had been intercepted in Southern California. When the cargo was checked, a large quantity of counterfeit stamps had been discovered.

online purchases. Once the initial sale is completed, however, victims are often lured to make future stamp purchases outside the Internet.

Another hint to what was going on was reported in Les Winick's *Linn's* insider column dated January 5. The significance was not noted at the time, but Winick reported that a hoard of 20,000 fake U.S. $1.80 Future Mail Delivery airmail souvenir sheets (Scott C 126) had been discovered in Australia. Winick commented that those sheets were a brazen counterfeit of a United States financial obligation, no different than a well-printed fake $5 bill.

Robinson promised to get back with *Linn's* as developments in the case allowed. It is not known if Inspector Robinson ever did this, but we would hear more about the new counterfeits that would be discovered.

On April 19, 2004, *Linn's* reported that another example of the counterfeit 37-cent Flag (Scott#3635) had been brought to their attention. This item appeared to have seen postal usage. This stamp had been affixed to a plain envelope that had been cancelled in Detroit on March 22. Actually this envelope had been mailed from one collector to another and the wave line cancellation indicated it had triggered a Post Office facer-canceller. There was a double cancellation on the envelope indicating that possibly this cancellation may have been forced?

Sent to *Linn's*, they finally had an example of this counterfeit stamp to examine. Under short wave UV light there was no evidence of phosphor tagging. They noted a legitimate stamp would exhibit a yellow-green glow. When the forged stamp was put under long wave UV the paper glowed bright white. The paper of a real stamp would not have reacted at all. Besides the lack of phosphor tagging, the major and most glaring point of identification they pointed out was the omission of the micro printed USPS in the upper left hand corner.

A point that *Linn's* would repeat in many articles was due to the number of contracted private printing sources used by the Postal Service, and the number of formats common stamps were printed in, identifying counterfeits going through the mail is difficult. A stamp collector might be able to pick out one variety from another, but to the man on the street they are indistinguishable. Actually, when it comes to identification, even collectors are often confused.

Once the existence of these counterfeits was reported in the philatelic press, numerous examples would be sent into *Linn's* for authentication. As a rule these items were found to be genuine. As Charles Snee would comment in Linn's, "The forged stamp is a dead ringer for the real thing. The colors are very close to those of a real stamp. The serpentine die-cuts on the three edges of the forged stamp are a near match compared with a real stamp, both in appearance and gauge."

The mystery of the double cancellation in this new counterfeit would be cleared up in the body of the *Linn's* article. When interviewed, the Michigan collector told the reporter that a collector friend, who had purchased some of these items, first told him these items were counterfeit. "So I asked my friend to send me one on cover." It arrived on March 20, but had not been postmarked, so he dropped it back in the mail, and when delivered a second time, it had been canceled. By doing this he had also just quadrupled its value as a collector's item.

The *Linn's* article, and many that would follow, went on to castigate the postal service philosophy of cost cutting in stamp production. They pointed out this not only impacted the body of the hobby, but more importantly negatively impacted the security of postal products and the revenue it would generate. "The appearance of well-executed 37-cent Flag knockoffs points out the glaring vulnerability of the U.S. Postal Service's stamp-printing methods, which rely on speed and economics of scale at the expense of quality printing and security." Offset-printed stamps may be cheap to produce, but unfortunately, they also create a tempting target for the counterfeiter. This makes it very hard to separate the good from the bad. Postal management seems not to grasp the reality that the "average honest man concept" as a protection of their revenue is now dead and buried.

Then, on August 9, *Linn's* reported yet another example of a fake 37-cent Flag counterfeit had surfaced. It was on a cover at a Jarnick auction in July. It was hammered down for $79. Again it was noted the stamp lacked the USPS micro printing, and was not phosphor tagged. "Apparently the missing tagging caused the automatic facer-canceller machine to reject the cover, and it was cancelled by a postal clerk with a roller-canceller." Jarnick also noted that the cover had been marked "Forgery" on the pack.

A new era had dawned in the area of postal counterfeiting.

Whether they knew it or not, *Linn's* in the March 15, 2004, issue presented a hint to what was going on:

> *Linn's* Insider columnist Les Winick reported January 5 that a hoard of 20,000 fake U.S. $1.80 Future Mail Delivery airmail souvenir sheets (Scott C126) was discovered in Australia. The sheet is a brazen counterfeit of a United States financial obligation, no different than a well-printed $5 bill.

That was just a hint of what was going on.

Then, in August 23, 2004, a new wrinkle appeared. This time the headline was "Forged 2002 Flag coil surfaces in California."

37-cent Flag Coil (nondenominational) Scott #3622

At some point during the year, forged examples of the 37-cent nondenominational (Scott #3622) were found in the mail coming from Bakersfield, Industry, and San Bernardino, California. Once again significant quantities of these items appeared to have been sold both on Internet auction sites and also eBay.

This time *Linn's* learned of the existence of this stamp from Postal Inspector Mike McCarthy. He was the public information officer for the Los Angeles Division. McCarthy stated, "I was alerted to mail bearing the forged coil stamps perhaps last summer or early fall. I don't know exactly when unused examples of the stamps were discovered, but significant volumes have been seized at this point."

He also gave good hints at how this counterfeit could be identified. The forged stamps bear a "2003" year date in the lower right corner, and looks like the stamp issued in 2002. Again the classic identification method is suggested. Place the questioned stamp next to a legitimate stamp and differences will be readily apparent. "The colors of the counterfeit stamps are not the same as real stamps. Besides the incorrect "2003" date, on copies of this stamp I have seen this incorrect date appear not in the bottom right margin, but slightly elevated so that it impinges on the lower right stamp design."

According to Inspector McCarthy, an administrative decision had been made regarding how letters bearing counterfeit stamps would be handled. They would be marked "Return to Sender –

Evidence of Counterfeit Postage," and then sent back to the mailer. This was a policy that I had previously argued against. My reasoning was simple. The mailers are the bread crumbs you can use to lead you back to the individuals behind the crime. Still I can understand the reasoning that must have occurred. You can be simply overwhelmed with the volume, and in the interests of saving manpower and time, you may be forced to do this. That this had been done gives an indication that a large number of counterfeits must have been found in the mail. It was argued that still all would not be lost. Along with the returned mailing piece was sent a letter from the inspectors requesting either the sender or mail recipient please inform the Inspection Service of any pertinent information. I could not help wondering just how many individuals beat down the authorities' door with information, or would then surrender any more counterfeits they had in their possession.

For the stamp collector this presents another point to ponder. If you find one of these envelopes bearing a counterfeit stamp and the sticker acknowledging its counterfeit nature – congratulations you have just been presented with a new philatelic treasure.

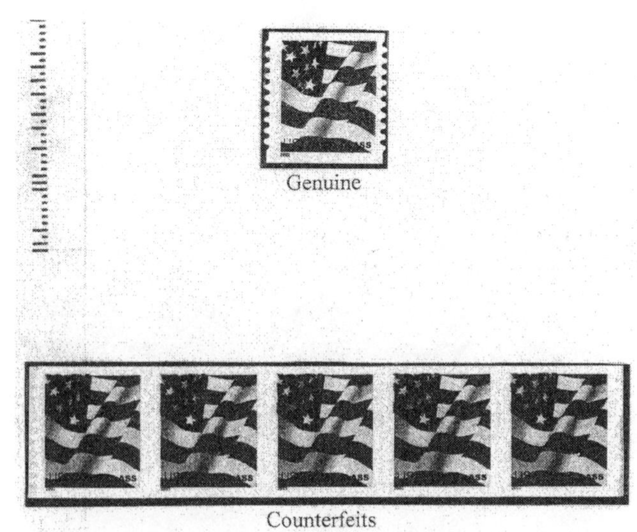

The 37-cent nondenominational stamp and counterfeits

37-cent Booklet Flag
Scott #3635

Then under the byline of Jay Bigalke, *Linn's* reported in the October 3, 2005, issue, new version of the 37-cent counterfeit had been identified. Stamp collector Zeb Vance, a resident of Florida, had purchased a mixture from a stamp dealer in Southern California. When he looked through his stamps he found what appeared to be a counterfeit of the 37-cent booklet Flag (Scott #3635). This stamp had die cuts on three sides. The straight edge on the top indicated that most likely it had come from a booklet pane of 20.

The new counterfeit is different from both of the earlier counterfeit flags reported in Linn's. Its separations are distinctly different from those of the authentic issue. The counterfeit's die cuts are approximately 11.5 instead of the correct 11.3 mm. Again this counterfeit does not have the micro printing security feature. Examining the stamp's image it was found that in duplicating both the design and the date the image was created by large dots. This indicates a low- resolution printing. Half-tone screen comes to mind. Again, this stamp is not tagged, and appears to have been printed on a glossy paper. Under long-wave UV the paper of the counterfeit was found to be very bright.

Information soon surfaced indicating that both nondenominated and denominated versions of the counterfeit Flag stamp were being found. Both existed in a coil format. The nondenominated stamp had the text "USA First Class" instead of 37 USA." Both versions were turning up in large quantities all across the United States.

On March 15, 2005, Wayne Youngblood wrote an article for the *Stamp Collector*. He presented a description of what he suspected was going on with the fake 37-cent Flag stamps. Wayne correctly described this as perhaps the largest United States counterfeiting case in recent decades. If anything this was an understatement. Wayne saw the significance of a statement Inspector Robinson had made. Robinson had said that multiple denominations – "up to the Express Mail rate – are being counterfeited." This was a topic that for the most part had been overlooked.

As Wayne described developments in the case, he noted that during the beginning weeks of 2005, lots began to appear in online auctions. Substantial quantities of mint stamps were being offered at significant discounts. He pointed out that unlike older issues that commonly are sold at a discount, these were current issues. They were being offered in fully sealed and shrink-wrapped decks complete with the deck identification cards. This is the exact same shipping and distribution format utilized by the government. Again Wayne made the observation that if anyone buying these stamps had any suspicion anything was wrong, they would more likely believe them stolen than counterfeit. After all, if you think about it, when was the last time the Treasury had a sale on $20 bills?

When these stamps were discovered, the Los Angeles Division of the Postal Inspection Service sent out a memo to alert postal employees. This is paraphrasing what Wayne reported: Samples of these counterfeits have been acquired and are described as being sold as standard $7.40 booklets of self-adhesive Flag stamps. To the naked eye, the booklets and the stamps they contain appear legitimate.

"Forensic analysis of two of the booklets revealed that they were unusually high-quality counterfeits produced by offset printing. The booklet covers were imprinted as $7.40 Flag stamps, stock #670990, B5555. In addition, processing plants in Los Angeles and Santa Ana, California, detected counterfeit 37-cent U.S. Flag stamps on envelopes mailed by specific businesses during a time frame that samples were being distributed to potential buyers. The exceptional quality and the reported quantity of these counterfeit stamp booklets present a serious threat to postal revenue."

It was apparent that thousands of counterfeit booklets had been produced, and were being used. Points of mailing were identified from coast to coast. These locations included New Jersey; Miami, Florida; Chicago, Illinois; Studio City, California; and Seattle and Bellevue, Washington. At Bellevue, one individual who had purchased stamps online, turned around and redeemed them at the Post Office. They were then put into the main stamp stock and resold to the public.

Just before I retired, I was involved with security issues relative to the then planned self- adhesive stamps. Other than ~~the fact that~~ I did not think highly of the proposed printing methods (offset), I fully supported the die cutting and adhesive program. My thought was that this would take the run-of-the mill counterfeiter out of the picture. My thinking had been this would require a whole new level of equipment to produce really authentic-looking postage. I did not recognize that the era of the computer, scanner and color printer was dawning. It was a totally wrong analysis on my part. I did not recognize that self-adhesive die cut paper stock was or soon would be readily available on the open market. Another thing I did not consider, just maybe there was someone or something else out there than the simple back room counterfeiter.

When I first heard about what was being identified as these new forgeries, my thought was that something significant was happening here. Everything I found in the general and philatelic press was screaming "overseas." This was only reinforced when I encountered some of the then current Canadian counterfeits. These were in booklet form and the only description appropriate was that they were a work of art. When I tried to run down information from dealers about these items, the only thing I heard was: "They are coming from overseas."

Now in the United States, I was looking at the three varieties of 37-cent counterfeits. Considering how they appeared, the quality of printing, their packaging, and how they were marketed – everything about these items screamed this was not some home grown back-room operation. I believe the mystery was solved in the *Linn's* issue of September 10, 2005: "FBI sting nets counterfeit U.S. Stamps."

A Criminal State?

Under Attack Only Nobody Told the Public

For more than eight years, the FBI had been working a particularly interesting case. Historically, organized crime had a very tight control of the docks on both the East and West coasts. Though the "Mob" had been knocked back on its heels, the docks were still an area targeted for corruption. The Bureau still kept these access points under heavy surveillance, and the New Jersey crime family had itself been targeted. Sometime around 1995, the word began to go around the docks that someone wanted to open a pipeline through various ports.

When it started, the Bureau probably had no idea how extensive or large this case would be. On the East Coast it was given the code name "Operation Royal Charm." Two agents began a long-term undercover operation where they played the role of freight expediters who could get things through the ports. They could avoid customs, take a cargo to a secure warehouse, and help facilitate its transportation to a final destination. In the end, the agents pulled off this most difficult, and long-term assignment. Finally, a point had arrived when it was decided to pull the plug.

Rivaling the plot of a Hollywood movie, they decided to stage a wedding for the two undercover agents. This was to take place on a yacht moored in Atlantic City, and it was only natural they would invite their criminal associates. When the 87 invited guests arrived, one by one they were arrested. Initially they would be charged with both counterfeiting and smuggling. Then, over the weekend an additional 59 individuals would be picked up at 11 other locations in the United States and Canada. The targeted cities were Atlantic City, Los Angeles, Las Vegas, Chicago and Philadelphia. The charges would soon be amended to reflect violations of the "Racketeering Influenced and Corrupt Organizations (RICO)" statutes. This involved dealing in counterfeit U.S. currency, narcotics trafficking, money laundering, conspiracy to defraud the United States, and illegal weapons trafficking. On the East Coast, the United States Attorney who had directed and would steer the prosecutions through the East Coast federal courts was Chris Christy, the current governor of New Jersey.

Identified as seized by the government was $4.4 million in counterfeit $100 bills, approximately one billion counterfeit Marlboro and Newport cigarettes, and several thousand dollars' worth of fake blue jeans. The drug seizure was also significant. There were hundreds of thousands of dollars' worth of ecstasy, methamphetamines and Viagra. Oh, and then as an afterthought it was acknowledged that also found was $700,000 in counterfeit Flag design stamps! Important to be remembered, these numbers only reflect what was seized on the East Coast when the arrests went down. This is an operation that had been going on from at least 1996, and many, many shipments had gone through before the government stopped the operation.

In the July 23, 2006, issue of the *New York Times Magazine*,

Stephen Mihn gave a little more detail on how this case had developed. On October 2, 2004, the container ship "Ever Unique" arrived in Newark, New Jersey from Yantai, China. One of the containers was transported to a warehouse. When it was cracked open, under a layer of toys, agents found counterfeit $100 bills worth more than $300,000. These were not some clumsily executed copies run off on a home computer. These items were what the authorities had previously identified as the Super Note. Two months later another ship arrived in Newark with $3 million in counterfeit dollars. In May of 2005, another ship arrived. This time it was in Long Beach, California with a shipment of $700,000 Super Notes. In Stephen Mihn's article he was simply identifying the counterfeit currency in those shipments. He did not document the other counterfeit items, most likely including postage stamps, which would have been included in those shipments. All of this contraband was allowed to go through because seizing the material would have tipped off the smugglers and compromised the government's investigation.

Mirroring what had occurred on the East Coast, a shadow investigation had been under way on the West Coast. Another agent had been able to infiltrate that operation. This was Special Agent Bob Hamer, an accomplished undercover agent who would work for over three years gaining the trust of the criminals involved. The West Coast case was just as significant as what was happening in the East, it just never received the same degree of press coverage that "Royal Charm" did. The code name for the West Coast operation was "Smoking Dragon." Just maybe the name gives you a hint of who was believed to be behind this criminal activity.

When the indictments came down in Los Angeles, 30 individuals would be scooped up. Unfortunately, the involvement of counterfeit postage stamps was never either documented or publicly accounted for. What would be publicized was the $1.2 million in counterfeit currency, $40 million in counterfeit cigarettes, and the extensive amount of counterfeit drugs and narcotics. Grabbing the public's attention was the "good-faith" shipment of a Chinese surface to air anti-aircraft missile (QW-2). This weapon had been shipped to the United States as an example of the military equipment they were contracting to ship to West Coast ports. These overseas suppliers had committed to providing $1 million worth of silenced pistols, submachine guns, assault rifles, and other weapons including rocket launchers. Do you really think this military equipment would have been provided without either official involvement or at least their connivance?

In Royal Charm the FBI had worked a joint investigation with the Postal Inspectors, the Secret Service, Customs, the RCMP, and selective local law enforcement. Because of the postal involvement on the East Coast, the counterfeit postage aspect had been well documented. On the West Coast there is no indication that the Inspection Service had been in the loop, yet it is firmly established that the West Coast ports were a pipeline for counterfeit stamps into the United States. None of the West Coast inspectors I searched out and spoke to professed to have any knowledge or involvement with that undercover operation. They just had the unenviable task of trying to run down those distributing the stamps on the street. The inspectors did make a number of arrests, but they were the worker bees.

The Super Bill

There is an obvious connection between the currency being seized and the counterfeit stamps being encountered across the United States. Being found in the same shipping container might be considered a real big hint. Then of course, once this material was in the United States, the same individuals were involved in the distribution of the same products. In the case of both the currency and the postage stamps, they were works of art.

When the Super bill first popped up, I heard a couple of different theories about the origin of this counterfeit bill. The first version was that there was a press in the Bakaa Valley in Lebanon that was producing them. Another popular theory was that they came from Iran. The story I heard was that just before the Shah fell, our government had shipped a brand spanking new intaglio press to that country. Much later, I would hear North Korea mentioned.

The bill itself is almost flawless. It had been printed on an intaglio press. The paper was manufactured to the same specifications as that used by our Treasury. In later models they were even using the new optical variable ink. The plate engraving was considered to be even superior to that executed by the Bureau of Engraving. This could only be done if it had State sponsorship and support. The thing that promptly comes to mind is the counterfeiting operation of Adolf Hitler during World War II.

A government report stated that the Super bill was first identified in the Philippines in 1989, and the Secret Service gave it the identification number of C-14342. A series of bills would be identified, all with the same basic characteristics. They would pop up across the world until they finally were identified in the United States. When questioned about the problem represented by the new counterfeit notes, the Treasury department would downplay its significance. It was stated that only $45 million in these bills had been identified within the United States. The only problem with this reasoning is that it does not take into consideration the possibly billions in bogus currency distributed in Europe, Eastern Europe, the Middle East and Asia.[52] Considering the quality of the counterfeit stamps that had been found and there being co-located with this counterfeit currency, it is reasonable to assume these items may have originated from the same source.

I would encounter the Super bill somewhere around 1990. One day I was called to the Dead Letter Office in St. Paul, Minnesota. They reported they were finding suspicious letters apparently coming from Lebanon. These were opened to find forwarding information, but instead found five or six crisp new $100 bills in these envelopes. Believing something was unusual here, I sent examples to the Secret Service crime laboratory for validation. After about three submissions, the word finally came back identifying these items as counterfeit.

Speaking to Inspector Robinson about his stamp investigation, he acknowledged when he began to investigate the new counterfeit stamps he had a similar experience. He sent examples of the 37-cent Flag to the Washington, D. C. Crime Laboratory and they reported back they were genuine. It was only after he made his third submission, and they took a real close look, suddenly they excitedly called back and said, "Yes, they are counterfeit."

---

52 It is estimated that three-quarters of the currency issued by the United States Treasury is not circulating in the United States but rather in other countries.

Where did the counterfeit currency and very possibly the stamp originate? The current general consensus, but very quietly voiced view, is North Korea. At the very least, from the beginning the thought had been this was an international criminal ring based in Southeast Asia. Then Daniel Glaser of the Treasury Department filed his report: "There is no question of North Korea's involvement. " They had been counterfeiting both our currency and stamps since the mid 1950s. Now as the new Super bills began to show up it was established that North Korea had purchased a Swiss-made intaglio printing press. This press had been installed in a high-security building called "Printing House 62" in Pyongsong, a city outside of Pyongyang. Then it was documented they had also purchased the O.V.I. color-shifting ink used on our new $100 bills from another Swiss company, SICPA.

In 1997, Hwang Jang Yop, a former secretary of the North Korean Workers Party and Kim Duk Hong, the head of the government trading company, defected. They provided additional information that on Changgwang Street in Pyongyang there is a barricaded compound that is the home of "Office 39." The purpose of this facility, besides legitimate enterprises, is to obtain hard revenue for the regime by overseeing counterfeit drug manufacturing, sales of missile technology, counterfeit cigarettes, and counterfeit currency. Most likely another target of their attention was postage stamps.

Then a report issued by the Congressional Research Service identified North Korea as the source of at least $45 million in counterfeit U.S. currency – the Super bill found in this country. This North Korean operation is identified as directly tied to criminal organizations in Japan, Taiwan, China, and Vietnam. This criminal enterprise is working closely with Chinese businesses, and Chinese banks have been used to deposit the hard money so generated. The congressional report simply identifies the DPRK (North Korea) as a "Criminal State." For those who would question why North Korea would be doing this activity, recently Condoleezza Rice made the comment that the words "rationality and North Korea should never be used in the same sentence."

It has been established that shortly after the Korean War, North Korea began to counterfeit U.S. postage stamps. At that time the thought was this was more for propaganda purposes than anything else. The general consensus was that nobody would be doing this simply to steal money. Then someone in the North recognized that hard income needed to be raised to support the government elite and it could be raised in this manner. It is believed that this is the driving force behind the production of counterfeit stamps, cigarettes, drugs and currency. It is also behind their export of missiles and nuclear technology. Supporting this view is a South Korean report identifying O Kuk Ryol, the Vice Chairman of the DPRK's National Defense Commission as responsible for directing counterfeiting operations in the North. This is not an insignificant person. He was identified as the facilitator behind the transfer of power to Kim Jong-il.

For North Korea, the counterfeiting of merchandise, drugs, currency and postage stamps is simply war by a different name. Besides supplying the North with hard currency that supports the regime, the object is to destroy Western economies. With North Korea this is national policy. With China, if supporting this activity is not national policy, the authorities are at least looking the other way. We are engaged in an economic war. The only problem is, nobody has told the American public.

Oh, just another gem I recently picked up. When the Postal Service decided to take stamp production away from the Bureau of Engraving and Printing, they threw it out on the free market. At some point a contract was awarded to one company in the U.S. that then subcontracted the stamp production to a company in Canada. They in turn subcontracted to a company in China. See where I am going here? If you do not want North Korea as the designated fall guy, I would strongly suggest another target – China. The suspicion is that they are involved in this activity right up to their eyeballs. It is very unlikely with state- sponsored industry that counterfeiting activity would be occurring without at least some degree of connivance from those in power. Oh, and then running the hard currency through Chinese banks does not hurt either.

Every year billions of dollars in counterfeit merchandise flows into this country. Much of this material originated in China. Now, tell me again why we wanted to sell and basically give up sovereignty over the Port of Los Angeles to the Chinese People's Army? Didn't the French, English and Germans basically force China to do the same thing to their ports back in the 1800s? How did this work out for the Chinese then? Maybe they think turnaround is fair play.

It is suspected that the Chinese are actively involved in the counterfeiting activity. In the world of computers and hacking, attacks on our industry, banking and military, at least 80% of these attacks have been identified as originating in China.

Could They be Back Again?

U.S. 39-cent Liberty and Flag

When the undercover FBI investigations went down on both the East and West coasts, numerous arrests were made. The Inspection Service also arrested many individuals they identified as distributing and selling those counterfeit stamps to the public. It is unlikely, however, this was the end of the problem. Unfortunately the only people arrested were the little fish. The source, the overseas operation, and the presses, had not been touched.

Jay Biglke in the February 12, 2007, issue of *Linn's* reported that counterfeit coils of the 39-cent Liberty and Flag stamp (Scott #3982) had been found. These stamps had again been identified being sold on eBay. Biglke described this as a dangerous counterfeit, a near-perfect copy of the original. These items were being sold in coil rolls of 100 stamps each.

Starting on January 4, 2007, it appeared that a single seller in New York began to sell these items in large auction blocks. This seller would generally offer five to 10 rolls at a time. The selling price was around $33 per coil roll. In one of his last listings he had posted the following:

> Attention if you are a stamp seller or are involved in philatelic activity, you are not allowed to purchase any rolls on this fixed price auction. You are considered strictly as competitors. Again, if you sell any type of stamps you are excluded from this auction.

As of January 25, *Linn's* identified more than 750 rolls of these stamps as having been sold. The individual who alerted *Linn's* to the existence of these counterfeits was Ron Maifeld, a stamp collector.

He also provided *Linn's* with examples of the stamps he purchased on eBay. Maifeld was president of the Plate Number Coil Collectors Club, and it was the lack of plate numbers that led to his conclusion these items were counterfeit: "On an authentic roll, plate No. S111 appears on every 14th stamp."

Again on these coil rolls there were no plate numbers.

Another identification point was the leader strip on the counterfeit coils. On the item he examined they did not match the leader strip used by the Sennett Company on the coils they supplied the Postal Service. On the counterfeit rolls this leader strip is blank. On the legitimate item it reads TOTAL = $39.00, FLAG/LIBERTY PSA COIL @ 100. Also noted, the individual stamps do not have phosphor tagging. Examined under short wave UV, the counterfeit emits no light. The die cuts on the vertical side of the fake measure 10.25, which exactly match the legitimate issue.

These stamps are a mystery. Due to both the quality of production and packaging employed, this counterfeit could be a continuation of the Korean 37-cent counterfeit operation. The packaging of the coils again mimicked legitimate coils put out by the government. At least that is what I thought until I encountered the next case.

From 2007 on, a series of counterfeit stamps popped up. When somebody has a good idea, there will be imitators. Some of these items may have originated overseas, others were obviously homegrown. On February 28, 2007, ABC news reported "Postal Inspectors Lick Counterfeit Stamp Ring." They reported how the inspectors had moved in on a printing operation being run out of an apartment on the Upper West Side of Manhattan. Working with the police, the inspectors had traced the sale of counterfeit 39-cent stamp rolls to this apartment.

When the search warrant was executed, the authorities seized hundreds of coil rolls of the Liberty Bell Flag stamp. These items were again found with packaging matching the USPS wrappers complete with barcodes. Items seized in the search included computer software, industrial sized cutting boards, three industrial printers and other printing supplies. Arrested at the printing plant were Hector Silvestre and Magaly Pickado.

This may have been home-grown, but once again it demonstrates the vulnerability of the U.S. Postal Service to exploitation. The authorities said the quality of the counterfeit stamps produced had been excellent. Interviewed, the men in custody stated these items had been destined to be sold on the Internet and at small grocery stores in New York. In a post – arrest interview, Silvestre acknowledged that he was producing about 150 coils each day. Before they were interrupted they had big plans for the future. Silvestre planned to expand the operation to begin running his production 24/7. He figured he could at least double their current production.

This counterfeit investigation had originally been triggered when employees at a New York Mail Distribution center noted that an inordinate number of 39-cent Liberty Flag stamps were being rejected by the facer-cancellers. At the end of the case, Tom Boyle, the Assistant Inspector in Charge of the New York office, stated that it was his belief that the U.S. Postal Service had suffered a loss of about $300,000.

Security vs. Retail

In every business there is a continual battle between customer service, and those who handle security. When you try to cut costs, one of the first expenses targeted frequently are those that relate to security. This conflict is every bit alive in the "New Postal Service" as it is with any business on Main Street. With the old Post Office, historically security was very much an issue. Stamps were seriously considered an obligation of the government so they went to great lengths to protect postal revenue. To make a new stamp the Post Office would go to the Bureau of Engraving and Printing, the same folks who make our currency, and say let's make a new stamp. This item would not only be a work of art, but it would also have many built-in security features.

From a philosophical point of view the Inspection Service would not tolerate the stealing of one penny. Back in 1972, I knew things were changing when after auditing the Houston Post Office we left after notating their postal accounts with the footnote,

"$50,000 unaccounted shortage."[53] The new Postal Service was more than willing to charge into the future. Today, stamp production is outsourced to private industry, and it would seem very little concern is given to the question of security. When revenue loss is experienced today, be it from theft or counterfeiting activity, postal management now referred to this as an acceptable rate of shrinkage.

The philosophy pushed by the bean counters is that the average citizen is honest and would not think of cheating or stealing. The shrinkage you experience is simply the cost of doing business. Sorry to tell you that is wrong. Just look at the scope of the stamp reuse problem discovered a few years ago. The only reason this is no longer an issue is that the use of stamps by the general public has so radically diminished. At just about every level you have the battle between retail and security. On the workroom floor postal supervisors are judged on meeting delivery standards, so is it a surprise that some supervisors would turn off the canceling machine to speed up the mail processing? From a security/revenue protection standpoint, there are days when one simply wants to beat one's head against the wall. I felt that way for years.

Counterfeiting used to be an art form with little financial or judicial risk. Today it is an everyday event practiced by numerous high school students with a computer. Most homegrown counterfeiting can be identified and combated once you begin to look for it. The same cannot be said when the counterfeits are made as part of national policy by another nation state. There is a reason the Secret Service now has an official or unofficial presence in many other countries. It is also why our currency is once again being redesigned.

The Postal Service is not running a multi-billion dollar deficit because of stamp counterfeiting, or other problems with revenue security, but counterfeiting/security issues have not helped. In a recent report to Congress the Postmaster General was forced to acknowledge that in the preceding year (2011) $134 million was lost to counterfeiting. That may be a low-ball figure. In a recent conversation with one inspector I was told that the "click and ship" program (another brainstorm from retail) has cost $100 million in fraud. The

53 Mind you this was about six months after a postal employee walked into the registry cage, opened the safe and then walked back out with $352,000.

concept itself may have been sound, but absolutely no attention or thought was given to security, abuse, and how to prevent fraud.

Even with our currency there is a problem. The Treasury has acknowledged that $45 million of the Super bills have been identified. What they fail to acknowledge is all the currency that has been dumped into Europe, Eastern Europe and Asia that people have buried in their back yard. Those bills will not be identified as counterfeit until it hits a bank, or the Federal Reserve. As European economies continue to contract, that day may not be far away. When those items are exposed as bogus, what impact will that have on faith in our currency?

Postal counterfeiting and revenue fraud have the attention of the Inspection Service, and now apparently some in postal management. It is something that has to be taken seriously, and if they start to look at the bottom line with stamps, meters, and permit mailing, just maybe they will begin to get their arms around other financial problems as well. Unfortunately, they do not have a good track record for doing this. Recently I heard the Postal Service has been using a new facer canceller. This machine is an optical reader. Reportedly it targets the image, not the phosphor tagging. There goes the one primary line of defense the Post Office still had left.[54]

Sometimes one simply has to ask, just what are the people making the decisions thinking? When it comes to stamp design and production, I have frequently asked myself, Are we trying to make the easiest item possible to duplicate?

It is known that stamp counterfeiting has not gone away. Once again we have amateur hour. On November 12, 2007, *Linn's* had the headlines: "Two fake U.S. 41-cent Flag coils discovered in Rhode Island." Paul Guertin, a Rhode Island stamp collector, had been going through mixtures of stamps. He was looking at thousands of Flag stamps when suddenly he noticed something odd. On a 41-cent nondenominational stamp (Scott #4133) the flag pool appeared to be black. He stated that it appeared to have a blurred appearance. He concluded it was a scanned image. The forgery had neither the micro printing nor the year date. Under UV light there was no luminescent

54 Rumor has it that those machines are now being replaced, but that they were installed to begin with speaks volumes.

tagging. The die cutting on this coil stamp measured 13, whereas on the original it would have been 11. This item had been postmarked from Providence, Rhode Island.

Counterfeit coil Scott 4133

Over the next two years various collectors would find other copies of counterfeit Scott #4133 in stamp mixtures. In the philatelic press there were no reports of whatever investigation the Inspection Service might have conducted. It was reported the ink composition appears to be constant from one stamp to another; cyan, magenta, yellow and black were used to produce the beige background to match the color of the original. The apparent die cut varied, with none of the counterfeits matching the authentic measurement of 11 mm.

In the September 14, 2009, issue of Linn's, it was reported that a new Flag counterfeit had been found. This was a copy of the Sennett Security Products stamp (Scott #4187), a 41-cent coil. Indicating that this counterfeit is possibly related to the earlier issue was the inks that were used. Again the background color was created with a mixture of cyan, magenta, yellow and black. Like before, the counterfeit had neither micro printing nor phosphor tagging. The flag pole on this counterfeit also matched the earlier versions in that it measured 21, rather than 22 as found on the legitimate stamp. As *Linn's* pointed out, it is important to note one of the contract printers of this stamp, Avery Dennison, was using gravure printing, which also does not use micro printing as a security feature. Obviously this will complicate the identification of counterfeit items. It is not known if the 41-cent flag counterfeit was ever traced back to its source or sources.

In what appears to be a totally unrelated case, it is my suspicion the Inspection Service was monitoring Internet sales of discounted stamp sales. On April 20, 2009, *Linn's* reported that "online stamp auctions had led postal inspectors to two new arrests." Apparently a postal clerk at Elkridge, Maryland had been identified in the theft of in excess of $600,000 in postage stamps. This employee had a confederate who handled selling the stolen stamps as discounted postage on eBay. In the Elkridge case you had internal theft by a postal employee and the Post Office had no idea this loss had occurred until the online sale of these stamps appeared. Chasing the stamp sales back to the source, inspectors determined they originated from internal theft. Back in the 1980s an annual loss of stamp stock to burglaries of Post Offices was $20 million each year.

Other Cases Appeared

In a Department of Justice news release dated November 24, 2009, they identified Icarus Dakota Ferris of selling $345,000 in counterfeit stamps. These items were similar to those produced through stamps.com. He was also selling these items as discounted postage on the Internet.

In April 2009, *Linn's* would announce that the Liberty Bell Forever stamp had been counterfeited. This was Scott #4125, the booklet pane gravure printing from Avery Dennison. This item was again being sold on eBay. Once again it was collector Ron Maifeld who made this discovery, and he was less than impressed by the effort. He described the die cuts as "atrocious." They were irregular and did not have a consistent gauge measurement. A knowledgeable collector might take note of this difference, but most likely the man on the street would not.

Besides the die cutting, the major identification characteristic was again the lack of tagging and the micro printing "Forever." On the legitimate stamp, the micro printing feature was located in the yoke of the bell. On the counterfeit this micro print is hard to make out, and it looks blurred and indistinct. On the stamp printed by Avery Dennison the micro print is clear and crisp. The blurred digital micro printing gives the production clue here. The Liberty Bell forever counterfeit is most likely computer generated, and not necessarily from a high-end scanner or printer.

Will this be the end of counterfeits? Not likely, so keep on looking. I do know there are at least two varieties of Purple Heart counterfeit stamps out there.

Final Thoughts

Our neighbors to the north have a rich history of stamp counterfeiting as well. This history almost rivals what has taken place in the United States. Being neighbors with a common border, criminal activity has frequently washed across the border going both ways. Being fully occupied trying to keep up with what occurred down here, I left reporting on those misadventures to the very able Canadian stamp authorities.

As related before, some time ago I knew something unusual was going on north of the border when I bought some spectacular Canadian counterfeits. When I received those items, my immediate response was, "oh my god." They were perfect and only an expert would have identified them as bad. One expert on all things Canadian is Richard Gratton. It was he who besides the stamps I had would identify three different booklet issues together. These items were the 49-cent Elizabeth, the $1.05 White Tail Deer, and the $1.40 Maple Leaf. For myself, all attempts to learn more about these items met a brick wall either from my stamp dealer friends or the RCMP.

Gratton in the *Fakes Forgeries Experts Journal*, number 14 issued in April 2011, identified new counterfeit issues. They were the Queen Elizabeth II booklet (issued January 2009), the Lighthouse booklet (issued May 2008), and the Vancouver Olympics booklet (issued 2009). These were all nondenominational permanent stamps. Gratton shares the same view of nondenominational stamps that I do: "This has to be one of the dumbest ideas that any postal bureaucrats ever came up with."

It is not known if these counterfeit stamps again go back to North Korea, but that is my suspicion. Gratton has also published a table documenting the number of counterfeit stamps a knowledgeable stamp collector had recently identified in a survey of incoming mail at one Montreal firm. Out of 26,758 envelopes he examined, he identified 176 counterfeits. The analogy here is the proverbial needle in the haystack. In this case this individual had found 176 needles where there should have been none.

It is my suspicion that the international counterfeiting activity I have been describing has not been limited to the United States and Canada. Consider the following: In 2007, $150,000 in counterfeit New Zealand stamps were intercepted at the Auckland, New Zealand International Mail Center. These were high-quality copies of the then current $1.50 and $3 denominations. They were in a sheet format and beautifully perforated. In Australia an unknown number of United States Purple Heart stamps were intercepted entering that country. In December 2011, it was reported that large quantities of counterfeit stamps were being sold on the Internet in the Netherlands. It is not known which stamp or stamps were the target of this attention. Authorities in Great Britain were kept busy with at least two large shipments of counterfeit stamps they intercepted while being smuggled into that country.

The battle is still going on in the United States. In 2012 I was told of a new case. It involved not only an attack on postal revenue, but in this case it also endangered people. As the story goes, mirror websites had been created. These websites look just like the legitimate websites normally used by the customers. People contact this site to place online drug orders. Correspondence has been sent back and forth with letters bearing counterfeit Purple Heart stamps. Drugs are sent to the unsuspecting customers with envelopes bearing counterfeit Express Labels. The drugs sent to the customers are counterfeit as well.

The way the authorities were alerted to this case was when one customer with a heart condition contacted the Post Office to inquire where his heart medications were. Who knows what the so-called medications supplied actually were, or how effective they would be for the unsuspecting sick customer.

In this, and other writing, I have tried to demonstrate not only how counterfeiting has evolved, but also how the investigative agencies have changed. The poster boy for that evolution is the FBI.

Historically, they were the agency everyone detested. They cooperated with nobody. A common joke was the most dangerous location was between the Bureau and a reporter. Things changed after the death of Hoover and his sycophants had left the scene. This was best demonstrated in the investigation of Operation "Royal Charm." The FBI was the lead agency, but just about every other federal agency along with state and local support took part. The success the Bureau had combating organized crime is monumental. In this they accomplished what many others only tried.

Successful criminal investigations take place in a news vacuum. There is a reason the Inspection Service was historically called the silent service, and the word secret is in Secret Service. The problem this generates is that the only time the public finds out the details of a crime is when a case goes to trial. That usually means some agent may have done something wrong, or at least there is a perceived legal issue. It also needs to be remembered that how a case may have been investigated years ago is not what would comply with legal standards today.

These have been fascinating stories to relate. I hope the reader found them both informative and entertaining. One thing to remember is that this story is far from over, and I hope the search for bread crumbs will go on, for as long as stamps have value, individuals will copy them. It is human nature.

32436187R00127

Made in the USA
Lexington, KY
19 May 2014